Happy Birthday ♥

3/11

May you always be found,

Walking with God .

Love. Mom

Walking with God

Talk to Him. Hear from Him. Really.

JOHN ELDREDGE

THOMAS NELSON
Since 1798

NASHVILLE DALLAS MEXICO CITY RIO DE JANEIRO

Published in Nashville, Tennessee, by Thomas Nelson. Thomas Nelson is a registered trademark of Thomas Nelson, Inc.

Published in association with Yates & Yates, www.yates2.com.

Thomas Nelson, Inc., titles may be purchased in bulk for educational, business, fund-raising, or sales promotional use. For information, please e-mail SpecialMarkets@ThomasNelson.com.

Unless otherwise noted, Scripture quotations are taken from the HOLY BIBLE: NEW INTERNATIONAL VERSION®. Copyright © 1973, 1978, 1984 by International Bible Society. Used by permission of Zondervan. All rights reserved.

Scripture quotations marked MSG are taken from *The Message* by Eugene H. Peterson, Copyright © 1993, 1994, 1995, 1996, 2000. Used by permission of NavPress Publishing Group. All rights reserved.

ISBN 978-1-4002-0290-4 (trade paper)

Library of Congress Cataloging-in-Publication Data

Eldredge, John.
   Walking with God / John Eldredge.
      p. cm.
   Summary: "Stories of becoming intimate and walking with God over the course of a year"
—Provided by publisher.
   ISBN 978-0-7852-0696-5 (hardcover)
   ISBN 978-1-4002-8005-6 (IE)
   1. Christian life. I. Title.
BV4501.3.E435 2007
248.4—dc22   2007041212

Printed in the United States of America
10 11 12 13 RRD 6 5 4 3

*For Stasi, with whom I have learned
nearly all of these lessons.*

Contents

Introduction

This is a series of stories of what it looks like to walk with God over the course of about a year.

It is our deepest need, as human beings, to learn to live intimately with God. It is what we were made for. Back in the beginning of our story, before the fall of man, before we sent the world spinning off its axis, there was a paradise called Eden. In that garden of life as it was meant to be, there lived the first man and woman. Their story is important to us because whatever it was they were, and whatever it was they had, we also were meant to be and to have. And what they enjoyed above all the other delights of that place was this—they walked with God. They talked with him, and he with them.

For this you and I were made. And this we *must* recover.

I've spent too many years trying to figure out life on my own.

Reading books, attending classes, always keeping an eye out for folks who seemed to be getting the hang of things. I'd notice that the neighbors' kids seemed to be doing well, and I'd think to myself, *What do they do that I'm not doing? Their kids are in sports. Maybe I should get mine in sports.* I'd walk away from a conversation with someone who seemed to be on top of the world, and afterward I'd think, *She seems so well-read. I'm not reading enough. I should read more.* I'd hear that a colleague was doing well financially, and quickly I'd jump to, *He spends time managing his money. I ought to do that.* We do this all the time, all of us, this monitoring and assessing and observing and adjusting, trying to find the keys to make life work.

We end up with quite a list. But the only lasting fruit it seems to bear is that it ties us up in knots. Am I supposed to be reading now, or exercising, or monitoring my fat intake, or creating a teachable moment with my son?

The good news is you can't figure out life like that. You can't possibly master enough principles and disciplines to ensure that your life works out. You weren't meant to, and God won't let you. For he knows that if we succeed without him, we will be infinitely further from him. We will come to believe terrible things about the universe—things like *I can make it on my own* and *If only I try harder, I can succeed.* That whole approach to life—trying to figure it out, beat the odds, get on top of your game—it is utterly godless. Meaning, entirely without God. He is nowhere in those considerations. That sort of scrambling smacks more of the infamous folks who raised the tower of Babel than it does of those who walked with God in the garden in the cool of the day.

In the end, I'd much rather have God.

You might have heard the old saying "Give someone a fish,

and you feed him for a day. Teach someone to fish, and you feed him for the rest of his life." The same holds true for life itself. If you give someone an answer, a rule, a principle, you help him solve one problem. But if you teach him to walk with God, well then, you've helped him solve the rest of his life. You've helped him tap into an inexhaustible source of guidance, comfort, and protection.

Really now, if you knew you had the opportunity to develop a conversational intimacy with the wisest, kindest, most generous and seasoned person in the world, wouldn't it make sense to spend your time with that person, as opposed to, say, slogging your way through on your own?

Whatever our situation in life—butcher, baker, candlestick maker—our deepest and most pressing need is to learn to *walk* with God. To hear his voice. To follow him intimately. It is the most essential turn of events that could ever take place in the life of any human being, for it brings us back to the source of life. Everything else we long for can then flow forth from this union.

But how do we get there? How do we learn to live with God, to walk with him each day in conversational intimacy? Over the years I've read with longing the stories of early disciples like Athanasius, who had the help of a spiritual giant like Anthony, or the Benedictines with Benedict, or the followers of Columba living with him on Iona, and I found myself wondering, *But where do people get that today?* Those stories feel like Aesop's fables. Charming, but archaic. I don't know anyone who lives in the same hut with a genuine spiritual counselor, mentor, father, or director with whom he can process the unfolding events of his life anytime he'd like. I know such fathers exist, and I pray they increase. But in the meantime, they are rare. Most of us haven't the option.

But we can still learn.

You might not have access to a master fly fisherman, but if you could watch someone cast who has been at it for a few years, you would learn a lot. When Stasi and I first married, we loved to hang out with couples who'd been hitched for a decade or two. There was so much to gain simply from hearing their experiences, the good and the bad. In truth, it was often the tales of their mistakes that helped us most. And so I've found that by describing my experiences and putting words to the things God is showing me, I can shed light on your experiences and put words to things God is showing you. In sharing these stories, I am in no way suggesting that this is the only way to walk with God. But as George MacDonald said, "As no scripture is of private interpretation, so is there no feeling in a human heart which exists in that heart alone, which is not, in some form or degree, in every heart."

And so what I offer here is a series of stories of what it looks like to walk with God over the course of about a year. I'm going to open my journals to you. Or at least part of them. The more helpful part, I hope. When Ernest Hemingway wrote *Green Hills of Africa* in 1935, he felt he was taking a worthy risk: "[I have] attempted to write an absolutely true book to see whether the shape of a country and the pattern of a month's action can, if truly presented, compete with a work of the imagination." How much more valuable might this be if we could share with one another the stories of our true encounters with God—not the mountaintop ones, but the everyday encounters, as they are lived out over a year.

Some of these stories will open up new horizons for you. That is certainly my hope. Learning to hear the voice of God may itself be a new frontier, and an exciting one, with unexpected joys around each new turn. You will no doubt come across lessons you've already learned, probably some better than I. But, you may have forgotten. We do forget even the most precious encounters we have with God. Perhaps I will help you to remember and recover what you might have lost. I may also help you to tell your own story as well, give you eyes to see what is unfolding and help you to set it down so that it doesn't slip away.

You'll notice that there aren't any chapters in this book. Life doesn't come to us that way, in neatly organized sections with helpful subheadings and footnotes. We don't get an outline for each new day, with summary points at bedtime. Life comes to us in a series of stories, over the course of time. There is something to be learned in every story. And there is something to be learned from seeing it unfold through the seasons—see the repetition of themes, the recurring attacks of the enemy, the hand of God in seemingly unrelated events. I think this format will allow you to pause along the way at those points where God is speaking to you, shedding light on your story, or teaching you something new. Pause there. Let that be the lesson for the day. Don't just plow through! Take your time, and let him speak.

I believe a deeper walk with God is available. I believe we can learn to hear his voice. But I'm well aware that it takes time, and we all need help *interpreting* the events of our lives, and what we are experiencing. So I have added another dimension to this book. At certain pivotal junctures along the way you will find references to the website walkingwithgod.net. On that site I provide further guidance, clarification and counsel through video. It's not exactly sharing a hut with Anthony or Benedict, but it will help a great deal in your walk with God.

I take some comfort in this quote from Frederick Buechner:

There is something more than a little disconcerting about writing your autobiography. When people have occasionally asked me what I am working on, I have found it impossible to tell them without an inward blush. As if anybody cares or should care. . . .

But I do it anyway. I do it because it seems to me that no matter who you are, and no matter how eloquent or otherwise, if you tell your own story with sufficient candor and concreteness, it will be an interesting story and in some sense a universal story. . . .

If God speaks to us at all other than through such official channels as the Bible and the church, then I think that he speaks to us largely through what happens to us, so what I have done in this book . . . is to listen back over what has happened to me—as I hope my readers may be moved to listen back over what has happened to them—for the sound, above all else of his voice. . . . [For] his word to us is both recoverable and precious beyond telling. (*Now and Then*)

prelude
summer
fall
winter
spring

learning to hear the voice of God

Listening to God

If only I had listened.

We have a family tradition of going out into the woods each year after Thanksgiving to cut down our Christmas tree. It's something we started when the boys were small, and over the years it became the event to help us inaugurate the Christmas season. We bundle the boys up and head off to the snowy woods on a Saturday morning. Stasi brings hot cocoa in a thermos; I bring the rope and saw. Inevitably, I think there's a better tree "just over the next hill," which is always one more hill away, and family members start peeling off and heading back to the car while I cut down a tree that's always three feet too tall and drag it a mile. It's all part of the tradition.

Now, you get a pretty funky-looking tree, sort of a Charlie Brown tree, when you go out to find one on your own. But it's *our* tree, with a story that goes along with it. We love it. Most of the time.

Last year we headed out for the tree the weekend *after* Thanksgiving weekend. There was new excitement to the adventure—we'd bought some land way out in the mountains, and this would be the first time we'd ever been able to cut a tree down on our own property. I envisioned a family hike on snowshoes up through the forest, hot drinks by the fire afterward, board games, rich memories. That's not exactly how it turned out.

A blizzard came upon us during the night and dumped about two feet of snow on the back roads. We decided we'd better get out while we could, but in the first five minutes of our journey home, we slid off into a ditch. It took us more than an hour to dig out. We had no shovel. We used the boys' plastic sled, with repeated failures. Finally, the only way we could get the Suburban to climb up onto the road was to have the whole family on the right side of the truck, outside on the running boards, riding it like a catamaran while I gunned it for all it was worth.

Slowly we made it back out to the highway. I got out to check the tree (we did get the tree, three feet too tall) and discovered that we now had two flat tires. Not one, but two. It was ten degrees outside, and the wind was howling down from the north, bringing the windchill to minus ten—as in ten below zero. I knew I had one spare tire, but not two. (Who carries two? Who gets two flat tires at the same time?) I did have a can of Fix-A-Flat—maybe that would get us into town. Nope, it was frozen. When I got out to deal with the situation, I left the flashers on to warn oncoming traffic of our condition. Now the battery was dead.

The word that comes to mind is *ordeal.* It was an ordeal.

And now here is my confession: we weren't supposed to go.

We'd prayed about the weekend, asking God when would be a good time to head out. This was the day after Thanksgiving (Friday), and both Stasi and I sensed God saying we were to go up the following day. But it didn't make sense to us. We were tired, and the boys wanted to see their friends. There were all sorts of "reasons" not to go, but more so there was that lingering unbelief that often passes for weariness, that thing in us that sort of whines, *Really? Do we really have to do this now, God?* So we ignored the counsel and went the following weekend. Now, the weekend God told us to go was a gorgeous weekend—no snow, sunny skies, no wind. The whole event would have been delightful.

But no. We had to do things our way.

How does the old hymn go? "Trust and obey, for there's no other way to be happy in Jesus, but to trust and obey." The whole ordeal could have been avoided had we simply listened.

The Power of Assumptions

I ran into an old acquaintance at the bookstore today.

Actually, I was nearly out the door when he called my name, so I turned back in to say hello and chat for a few moments. He seemed . . . not well. Half the man he used to be. I wondered why. I expected him to say that he had suffered some major loss. A loved one, I feared. Or maybe it was a prolonged illness. Not that he was visibly deteriorating as some do in the late stages of cancer. But there was something about his countenance, a loss of some essential part of himself. You know the look. Many people have it, actually. It's a confused and disheartened look. As we talked, it became clear that he had simply been eroded by a number of confusing years strung together by disappointment.

As I left the store, I found myself thinking, *He held such promise. What happened?*

It has to do with assumptions.

He assumed that God, being a loving God, was going to come through for him. In the sense of bless his choices. His ministry. Make his life good. He looked sort of dazed and hurt that it hadn't happened. He was trying to put a good face on it, but you could see that he had lost heart. This may be one of the most common, most unquestioned, and most naive assumptions people who believe in God share. We assume that because we believe in God, and because he is love, he's going to give us a happy life. A + B = C. You may not be so bold as to state this assumption out loud—you may not even think you hold this assumption—but notice your shock when thing don't go well. Notice your feelings of abandonment and betrayal when life doesn't work out. Notice that often you feel as though God isn't really all that close, or involved, feel that he isn't paying attention to your life.

Now, it's not fair to diagnose someone else's life without having some intimate knowledge of their situation, the story leading up to it, and what God is after. But I *do* have enough information to say that this man assumed the Christian life was basically about believing in God and doing good. Be a good person. That's good. That's a beginning. But it's just a beginning. It's sort of like saying that the way to have a good friendship is not to betray the other person. That will certainly help. You certainly want to have that going. But there's a whole lot more to friendship than simply not committing a betrayal, wouldn't you say? I know this fellow also holds the assumption that God doesn't really speak to his children. And so, when he found himself assaulted and undermined by all that had unfolded in his life, he had no source of guidance or explanation. It was sad to see the toll it had taken.

I left the store thinking about assumptions—how they are either helping us or hurting us, every single day of our lives. Our assumptions control our interpretation of events, and they supply a great deal of the momentum and direction for our lives. It's important that we take a look at them. And life will provide hundreds of opportunities to take a look at our assumptions in a single week. Especially as we walk with God.

I'll tip my hand to one assumption I am making. I assume that an intimate, conversational walk with God is available, and is meant to be normal. I'll push that a step further. I assume that if you *don't* find that kind of relationship with God, your spiritual life will be stunted. And that will handicap the rest of your life. We can't find life without God, and we can't find God if we don't know how to walk intimately with him. A passage from the gospel of John will show you what I'm getting at. Jesus is talking about his relationship with us, how he is the Good Shepherd and we are his sheep. Listen to how he describes the relationship:

> "I tell you the truth, the man who does not enter the sheep pen by the gate, but climbs in by some other way, is a thief and a robber. The man who enters by the gate is the shepherd of his sheep. The watchman opens the gate for him, and the sheep listen to his voice. He calls his own sheep by name and leads them out. When he has brought out all his own, he goes on ahead of them, and his sheep follow him because they know his voice." . . .
>
> "Whoever enters through me will be saved. He will come in and go out, and find pasture. The thief comes only to steal

and kill and destroy; I have come that they may have life, and have it to the full." (John 10:1–4, 9–10)

The sheep live in dangerous country. The only way they can move securely in and out and find pasture is to follow their shepherd closely. Yet most Christians assume that the way to find the life God has for us is to (A) believe in God, (B) be a good person, and (C) he will deliver the rest. A + B = C. But Jesus says no, there's more to the equation. I *do* want life for you. To the full. But you have to realize there is a thief. He's trying to destroy you. There are false shepherds too. Don't listen to them. Don't just wander off looking for pasture. You need to do more than believe in me. You have to stay close to me. Listen to my voice. Let me lead.

Now there's a thought: if you don't hold the same assumptions Jesus does, you haven't got a chance of finding the life he has for you.

Does God Still Speak?

I was talking on the phone yesterday with a young woman who was interviewing me for an article of some sort. She asked what this book was about, and I tried to explain it in this way: "This is a sort of tutorial on how to walk with God. And how to hear his voice." I told her several stories (including the one about the Christmas tree ordeal). There was a long pause, that pregnant sort of pause that tells me I've just hit upon a great need and a great doubt. Finally, she asked, "What do you say to people who say, 'God isn't that intimate with us?'" I had a hunch—it was something in the tone of her voice—that she hadn't experienced the Christian life in the ways I was describing. Maybe because she'd never been told this is available; maybe it's as simple as the fact that no one had ever shown her how.

Is God really that intimate with us? That's a good place to begin.

It might seem trivial that I'm bothering the God of the universe with a family outing for a Christmas tree. Does God really care about that kind of stuff? Is he really that intimate with us? Let's start with this much—God certainly knows *us* that intimately.

> O LORD, you have searched me
>   and you know me.
> You know when I sit and when I rise;
>   you perceive my thoughts from afar.
> You discern my going out and my lying down;
>   you are familiar with all my ways.
> Before a word is on my tongue
>   you know it completely, O LORD.
>
> You hem me in—behind and before;
>   you have laid your hand upon me.
> Such knowledge is too wonderful for me,
>   too lofty for me to attain.
>
> Where can I go from your Spirit?
>   Where can I flee from your presence?
> If I go up to the heavens, you are there;
>   if I make my bed in the depths, you are there.
> If I rise on the wings of the dawn,

if I settle on the far side of the sea,
even there your hand will guide me,
    your right hand will hold me fast.

If I say, "Surely the darkness will hide me
    and the light become night around me,"
even the darkness will not be dark to you;
    the night will shine like the day,
    for darkness is as light to you.

For you created my inmost being;
    you knit me together in my mother's womb.
I praise you because I am fearfully and wonderfully made;
    your works are wonderful,
    I know that full well.
My frame was not hidden from you
    when I was made in the secret place.
When I was woven together in the depths of the earth,
    your eyes saw my unformed body.
All the days ordained for me
    were written in your book
    before one of them came to be.

How precious to me are your thoughts, O God!
    How vast is the sum of them!
Were I to count them,
    they would outnumber the grains of sand.
When I awake,
    I am still with you.

(Psalm 139:1–18)

Whatever else we might believe about intimacy with God at this point, the truth is that God knows us *very* intimately. He knows what time you went to bed last night. He knows what you dreamed about. He knows what you had for breakfast this morning. He knows where you left your car keys, what you think about your aunt, and why you're going to dodge your boss at 2:30 today. The Scriptures make that very clear. You are known. Intimately.

But does God seek intimacy *with* us?

Well, start at the beginning. The first man and woman, Adam and Eve, knew God and talked with him. And even after their fall, God goes looking for them. "Then the man and his wife heard the sound of the LORD God as he was walking in the garden in the cool of the day, and they hid from the LORD God among the trees of the garden. But the LORD God called to the man, 'Where are you?'" (Genesis 3:8–9). What a beautiful story. It tells us that even in our sin God still wants us and comes looking for us. The rest of the Bible continues the story of God seeking us out, calling us back to himself.

The LORD is with you when you are with him. If you seek him, he will be found by you. (2 Chronicles 15:2)

I will give them a heart to know me, that I am the LORD. They will be my people, and I will be their God, for they will return to me with all their heart. (Jeremiah 24:7)

This is what the LORD Almighty says: "Return to me," declares the LORD Almighty, "and I will return to you," says the LORD Almighty. (Zechariah 1:3)

Come near to God and he will come near to you. (James 4:8)

Let us draw near to God. (Hebrews 10:22)

Intimacy with God is the purpose of our lives. It's why God created us. Not simply to believe in him, though that is a good beginning. Not only to obey him, though that is a higher life still. God created us for intimate fellowship with himself, and in doing so he established the goal of our existence—to know him, love him, and live our lives in an intimate relationship with him. Jesus says that eternal life is to know God (John 17:3). Not just "know about" like you know about the ozone layer or Ulysses S Grant. He means know as two people know each other, know as Jesus knows the Father—intimately.

But does God speak to his people?

Can you imagine any relationship where there is no communication whatsoever? What would you think if you met two good friends for coffee, and you knew that they'd been at the café for an hour before you arrived, but as you sat down and asked them, "So, what have you been talking about?" they said, "Nothing." "Nothing?" "Nothing. We don't talk to each other. But we're really good friends." Jesus calls us his friends: "I'm no longer calling you servants because servants don't understand what their master is thinking and planning. No, I've named you friends because I've let you in on everything I've heard from the Father" (John 15:15 MSG).

Or what would you think about a father if you asked him, "What have you been talking to your children about lately?" and he said, "Nothing. I don't talk to them. But I love them very much." Wouldn't you say the relationship was missing something? And aren't you God's son or daughter? "Yet to all who received him, to those who believed in his name, he gave the right to become children of God" (John 1:12).

Now, I know, I know—the prevailing belief is that God speaks to his people *only* through the Bible. And let me make this clear: he does speak to us first and foremost through the Bible. That is the basis for our relationship. The Bible is the eternal and unchanging Word of God to us. It is such a gift, to have right there in black and white God's thoughts toward us. We know right off the bat that any other supposed revelation from God that contradicts the Bible is not to be trusted. So I am not minimizing in any way the authority of the Scripture or the fact that God speaks to us through the Bible.

However, many Christians believe that God *only* speaks to us through the Bible.

The irony of that belief is that's not what the Bible says.

The Bible is filled with stories of God talking to his people. Abraham, who is called the friend of God, said, "The LORD, the God of heaven, who brought me out of my father's household and my native land and who spoke to me . . ." (Genesis 24:7). God spoke to Moses "as a man speaks with his friend" (Exodus 33:11). He spoke to Aaron too: "Now the LORD spoke to Moses and Aaron about the Israelites" (Exodus 6:13). And David: "In the course of time, David inquired of the LORD. 'Shall I go up to one of the towns of Judah?' he asked. The LORD said, 'Go up.' David asked, 'Where shall I go?' 'To Hebron,' the LORD answered" (2 Samuel 2:1). The Lord spoke to Noah. The Lord spoke to Gideon. The Lord spoke to Samuel. The list goes on and on.

I can hear the objections even now: "But that was different. Those were special people called to special tasks." And we are not special people called to special tasks? I refuse to believe that. And I doubt that you want to believe it either, in your heart of hearts.

But for the sake of the argument, notice that God also speaks to "less important" characters in the Bible. God spoke to Hagar, the servant girl of Sarah, as she was running away. "She gave this name to the LORD who spoke to her: 'You are the God who sees me,' for she said, 'I have now seen the One who sees me'" (Genesis 16:13). The God who sees even me. How touching. In the New Testament, God speaks to a man named Ananias who plays a small role in seven verses in Acts 9:

> The Lord called to him in a vision, "Ananias!"
>
> "Yes, Lord," he answered.
>
> The Lord told him, "Go to the house of Judas on Straight Street and ask for a man from Tarsus named Saul. . . ."
>
> "Lord," Ananias answered, "I have heard many reports about this man and all the harm he has done to your saints in Jerusalem. And he has come here with authority from the chief priests to arrest all who call on your name."
>
> But the Lord said to Ananias, "Go!" (vv. 10–15)

Now, if God doesn't *also* speak to us, why would he have given us all these stories of him speaking to others? "Look—here are hundreds of inspiring and hopeful stories about how God spoke to his people in this and that situation. Isn't it amazing? But you can't have that. He doesn't speak like that anymore." That makes no sense at all. Why would God give you a book of exceptions? *This is how I used to relate to my people, but I don't do that anymore.* What good would a book of exceptions do you? That's like giving you the owner's manual for a Dodge even though you drive a Mitsubishi. No, the Bible is a book of *examples* of what it looks like to walk with God. To say that he doesn't offer that to us is just so disheartening.

It is also unbiblical. The Bible teaches that we hear God's voice:

> He wakens me morning by morning,
>> wakens my ear to listen like one being taught. (Isaiah 50:4)

> For he is our God
>> and we are the people of his pasture,
>> the flock under his care. (Psalm 95:7)

> Today, if you hear his voice,
>> do not harden your hearts. (Psalm 95:7–8)

"The man who enters by the gate is the shepherd of his sheep. The watchman opens the gate for him, and the sheep listen to his voice. He calls his own sheep by name and leads them out. When he has brought out all his own, he goes on ahead of them, and his sheep follow him because they know his voice. . . .

"I am the good shepherd; I know my sheep and my sheep know me—just as the Father knows me and I know the Father—and I lay down my life for the sheep. I have other sheep that are not of this sheep pen. I must bring them also. They too will listen to my voice, and there shall be one flock and one shepherd." (John 10:2–4, 14–16)

We are his sheep. Jesus says that his sheep hear his voice. "Here I am! I stand at the door and knock. If anyone hears my voice and opens the door, I will come in and eat with him, and he with me" (Revelation 3:20). Jesus is speaking. He makes an offer. Who is the offer for? "Anyone." That would include you. What does Jesus say will happen? "Hears my voice." As in, hear his voice. And if we respond to his voice and his knocking, what will Jesus do? "I will come in and eat with him, and he with me." Sharing a meal is an act of communion, an offer of friendship. Jesus wants to pull up a chair, linger at our table, and converse with us. He offers to be intimate with us. What could be clearer? We are made for intimacy with God. He wants intimacy with us. That intimacy requires communication. God speaks to his people.

For more on this come to walkingwithgod.net

But What About Me?

Back to the interview.

Finally, we got down to the real issue. The young woman then asked, "What do you say to people who say, 'I don't hear God like that?'"

Okay. Now that's different. It's one thing to say, "God doesn't speak to his people." It's another thing to say, "I don't hear God speaking to *me*." This is what was fueling all her objections—*she* doesn't hear God like that. I felt bad for her. Here she had embraced all these theological assumptions as to why God doesn't speak to his people because *she* hasn't experienced God speaking to her. For one thing, if you've been taught that God doesn't speak to you, then you're probably not going to be listening for his voice. This all comes down to what kind of relationship you think God offers.

"It takes time," I said. "It's something we learn. Name one thing in your life that you really enjoy doing that didn't require practice to get there."

If you want to make music, you have to learn how to play an instrument. And in the beginning, it doesn't sound too good—all the squawks and squeaks and bad timing. You really *are* on your way to making music. It just sounds like you're strangling a pig. If you stick with it, something beautiful begins to emerge. Or how about snowboarding—learning to do that is really awkward at first. You fall down a lot. You feel like an idiot. But if you hang in there, you come to enjoy it. You get better. It starts to feel natural. That's when it becomes fun. This holds true for anything in life.

Including our walk with God. It takes time and practice. It's awkward at first, and sometimes we feel stupid. But if we hang in there, we do begin to get it, and as it becomes more and more natural, our lives are filled with his presence and all the joy and beauty and pleasure that come with it.

It is something to be learned.

And it is worth learning.

So there—you have my first assumption. An intimate, conversational walk with God is available. Is normal, even. Or, at least, is *meant* to be normal. I'm well aware that a majority of people do not enjoy that . . . yet. But it is certainly what God desires and what he offers. My assumption is based on the nature of God and the nature of man made in his image. We are communicators. My assumption is also based on the nature of relationship—it requires communication. It is based on the long record of God speaking to his people of various ranks in all sorts of situations.

And finally, it is based on the teachings of Jesus, who tells us that we hear his voice.

Now for assumption number two.

What Is God Up To?

I'm sitting in front of my computer this morning, my finger frozen over the left-click button on the mouse.

My e-mail program is asking me, "Are you sure you want to delete this message?" And I'm not so sure. It is *such* a good e-mail. It's incontestable. Undeniable. It's long overdue. Someone has ticked me off (details to remain undisclosed because they will probably read this book), and I've written what I feel to be is a very honest, straightforward, somewhat shaming and altogether irrefutable reply. I'm about to hit the Send button with the same satisfaction you see on the face of a player who gets to slam dunk a ball he stole on a fast break during the Final Four. This is going to be so good.

Then God says, *Don't do it.*

Don't do it?! Awww. Something in me sinks. The ref just blew a whistle. There's a foul on the play. Dang. It was going to be so good. It was deserved. *Why can't I send this?* I don't need for God to reply. I know why. The fact that I've found the whole process so utterly delicious tells me why. (You know that delicious. You have these moments too—those conversations you have in your head where you are brilliant and the other person is speechless.) I can sense the Spirit saying, *It won't do any good. They aren't in a place to hear it. Let it go.*

A long pause. A deep sigh. Things are shifting down inside. I am accepting more than guidance here. I am accepting change.

Down in my soul where the juncture of my will and my heart meet, I am accepting transformation. I click Yes and let the whole thing go.

Jesus says that as our Good Shepherd, he is leading us. What an encouraging thought. Jesus is leading you, and he is leading me. He is shepherding us. I can feel something in my heart loosening even now as I consider this. Okay. I don't have to make life happen on my own. Now, if Christ takes it upon himself to lead, then our part is to follow. And you'll find that it helps a great deal in your following if you know what God is up to. True, we may not know *exactly* what God is up to in this or that event in our lives. "Why didn't I get the job?" "How come she won't return my calls?" "Why haven't my prayers healed this cancer?" I don't know. Sometimes we can get clarity, and sometimes we can't.

But whatever else is going on, we can know this: God is always up to our transformation.

> God knew what he was doing from the very beginning. He decided from the outset to shape the lives of those who love him along the same lines as the life of his Son. The Son stands first in the line of humanity he restored. We see the original and intended shape of our lives there in him. After God made that decision of what his children should be like, he followed it up by calling people by name. After he called them by name, he set them on a solid basis with himself. And then, after getting them established, he stayed with them to the end, gloriously completing what he had begun. (Romans 8:29–30 MSG)

God has something in mind. He is deeply and personally committed to restoring humanity. Restoring you. He had a specific man or woman in mind when he made you. By bringing you back to himself through the work of Jesus Christ, he has established relationship with you. And now, what he is up to is restoring you. He does that by shaping your life "along the same lines as the life of his Son." By shaping you into the image of Jesus. You can be confident of this. It's a given. Whatever else might be going on in your life, God always has his eye on your transformation.

This is good news, by the way. All of the other things we long for in life—love and friendship, freedom and wholeness, clarity of purpose, all the joy we long for—it all depends on our restoration. You can't find or keep good friends while you are still an irritating person to be around. And there is no way love can flourish while you are still controlling. You can't find your real purpose in life while you're still slavishly serving other people's expectations of you. You can't find peace while you're ruled by fear. You can't enjoy what you have while you're envying what the other guy has. On and on it goes.

God wants us to be happy. Really. "I have come that they may have life, and have it to the full" (John 10:10).

But he knows that in order for us to be truly happy, we have to be whole. Another word for that is *holy*. We have to be restored.

Think of it this way—think of how you feel when you really screw things up. The look on your son's face as you yell at him. The distance that has grown between you even though you apologized. For the hundredth time. How it tears you up inside to indulge in romantic fantasies about someone else's spouse. You want that, but you don't want that, but you wish you could, but you really don't, and why is this going on inside? The guilt you feel when you lie straight-faced to a friend. And they find out.

The hours you've wasted harboring resentment. The embarrassment of your addictions. You know what plagues you.

Now, what would it be like to never, ever do it again? Not even to struggle with it. What would your life be like if you were free of all that haunts you?

Oh, the joy, the utter relief it would be to be transformed. That in itself would be more happiness than most of us ever experience. And—as if that were not enough—it would free us to live the life God has for us to live.

My friends, this is what God's up to. This is where our Shepherd is headed. Whatever else is going on in our lives, *this* is going on. He is committed to our transformation. So, if this is what God's up to, wouldn't it make sense that we be more intentional in partnering with him in our transformation? Part of me wishes I could have sent the e-mail. But the deeper, truer part of me is relieved that God stopped me. It would have hurt that person. I would have regretted it later. It would have created a crisis that would have taken hours of emotional energy to undo. I can't begin to number the disasters God has averted like that—the things he's stopped me from saying, the choices I would have made had he not intervened.

I want to walk with God.

summer

fall

winter

spring

a time of restoration and renewal,
and for finding our way back to joy

Slowing Down to Listen

This story actually begins back in June, with the first day of summer vacation.

I'm sitting on the porch of our cabin listening to the rain on the tin roof and watching it fall on all my plans for the day. I cannot hike. I cannot do chores. I cannot fish. The mud is so deep, I cannot drive anywhere. I'm trapped. Pinned down. With myself and God. There is nothing I can do but pay attention to what surfaces inside of me when I cannot charge into the day. I *am* paying attention, my journal on my lap, and this is what I begin to write:

I am tweaked again.

Royally flippin' tweaked.

I'm so tired and wrung, my body hurts from being tired.

Or hurts at the first chance to let down and be tired.

Granted, it has been a hard year. So much going on, so much

required. But God is after something. As I journal, I feel like a prisoner writing his confession.

And I know why I'm tweaked.

I'm tweaked from pushing.

Pushing, pushing, always pushing.

This pushing is such a way of life for me, I barely know how to live otherwise. I'm always working on something. Trying to make life better for me or for someone else. It feels like I heave myself at life. Always looking for some way to improve things. I come up here to the ranch to rest, and in the first ten minutes of quiet, here is where my mind goes: *I ought to teach Sam how to cast a fly rod. We ought to finish that back fence. I ought to work with the horses every day we are here. I could paint the door now. Better look at that topo map for my trip with Luke in August. Make a plan.*

Jesus, have mercy.

This rain is a mercy. I am forced to stop. With a bit of pouting, I begin to accept that this deluge is from God. I cannot live my life like this—always working on something. Trying to make life better. Pushing. It's the first day of my vacation, but I can't enjoy it because of the condition I'm in. And I did this to myself. I'm frayed like an old rope because of the way I live my life. And I've got a pretty good sense that this isn't the life God would have me live. I'm pretty sure there isn't a verse that goes, "He leadeth me to utter exhaustion; he runneth me ragged." In fact, doesn't Jesus say something about his yoke is easy and his burden light? Maybe I have some other yoke on me than the yoke of Christ.

Did I really need to take all those trips this year? *Really?* Did I really have to come through for everyone I felt compelled to come through for? *Really?* Here is the embarrassing question: did

I even ask God about those things? Now, I know, I know—our lives seem so inevitable. There's always a reason. There's always a defense. "But I *have* to live like this! If I didn't carry the world on my shoulders—who would?"

Drip. Drip. Drip. This downpour shows no signs of letting up. It is as persistent as the Spirit behind it.

Trapped on the porch, I know the issue is far bigger than this vacation. I know that full well. The issue is the way I live my life. And forced for a few moments to stop, I also know that I don't want to live like this. The very things I'm doing to try to make life happen—all those things that feel so inevitable and unavoidable—are draining me and preventing me from finding the life God offers. If you're about to run out of gas, the best thing to do is slow way down to conserve fuel so that you can make it to the next station. What I do is gun it. Put the pedal to the metal. No wonder God had to *command* us to rest. We wouldn't do it otherwise. Even with the command, we don't really do it.

Sitting here on the porch with God, I return to what I have forgotten—that there is a *life* out of which everything else flows. A life that comes to us from God. Jesus gave us the example of the vine and the branches. He is the vine, we the branches (John 15:5). The essential point of the imagery is that *life* flows from the vine through the branches, and only then do we get fruit. The branches are merely channels. They cannot make abundance happen. The branches need life to bring forth all the joy those grapes offer—the feasting, the wine, the merrymaking after the harvest. That life does not exist in the branches themselves. They—we—have to get it from another source. From God.

Now, rest is just one of the ways we receive the life of God. We stop, set all of our busyness down, and allow ourselves to be replenished. This is supposed to happen regularly. The original prescription was weekly. So why does rest feel like a luxury? Seriously, it feels irresponsible. We think we can drive ourselves like oxen fifty weeks a year, resurrect in a two-week vacation, then go back and do it all again. That is madness. My pushing and striving cut me off from the life I so desperately need. I don't even think to stop and ask, *Is this what you'd have me do, Lord? Do you want me to paint the bathroom? Volunteer at church? Stay late at work?*

So God sends this downpour to keep me from squandering my vacation by running like a greyhound. He loves me too much to leave me to my own devices.

I'm back to the shepherd and the sheep. When the sheep follow the shepherd, they find pasture. They find life. Life doesn't just magically come to us. We have to make ourselves available to it. There is a lifestyle that allows us to receive the life of God. I know that if I will live more intimately with Jesus and follow his voice, I will have a much better chance of finding the life I long for. I know it. If I will listen to his voice and let him set the pace, if I will cooperate in my transformation, I will be a much happier man. And so a new prayer has begun to rise within me. I am asking God, *What is the life you want me to live?*

If we can get an answer to that question, it will change everything.

On Learning to Listen

We are invited to become followers of Jesus.

Not just believers. *Followers.* There is a difference.

Follower assumes that someone else is doing the leading. As in "He calls his own sheep by name and leads them out. . . . He goes on ahead of them, and his sheep follow him because they know his voice" (John 10:3–4). The Bible invites us to an intimacy with God that will lead us to the life we are meant to live. *If* we will follow him. "I will instruct you and teach you in the way you should go; / I will counsel you and watch over you" (Psalm 32:8). God promises to guide us in the details of our lives. In fact, the psalm continues, "Do not be like the horse or the mule, / which have no understanding / but must be controlled by bit and bridle / or they will not come to you" (v. 9).

What would it be like to yield to Christ in the details of our lives? What would it be like to follow his counsel and instruction in all the small decisions that add up to the life we find ourselves living?

It would be . . . amazing.

I think we would find ourselves saying, as David did, "You have made known to me the path of life" (Psalm 16:11). This is the privilege and the joy of sheep that belong to a good shepherd. He leads them well. He leads them to life. So, back to the question, *What is the life you want me to live?* It is a good question— maybe one of the most important questions we could ever bring to God. He created us, after all. He knows why. He knows what is best for each of us. If we could learn from him the life he wants us to live—the details, the pace of life, the places we are to invest ourselves and the places we are not to—we would be in his will. And there we would find life.

But it's too big a question to ask. I find I have to start with something smaller.

This weekend, the first of our summer vacation, my simple question was, *What would you have us do: should we go to the ranch or stay home?* (The ranch for us is a place of rest and restoration. At least that's what it is supposed to be.) I knew I had to start there, with one simple question.

This is step one in learning to listen to the voice of God: ask simple questions. You cannot start with huge and desperate questions, such as, "Should I marry Ted?" or "Do you want me to sell the family business tomorrow?" or "Do I have lung cancer?" (Paranoia rarely enables me to hear God's voice.) That's like learning to play the piano by starting with Mozart, learning to ski by doing double black diamonds. There is way too much emotion involved, too much swirling around in our heads. I find that to hear the voice of God, we must be in a posture of quiet surrender. Starting with small questions helps us learn to do that.

Remember the story of the prophet Elijah after his triumph on Mount Carmel? He ran and hid in a cave. And there God spoke to him.

> The LORD said, "Go out and stand on the mountain in the presence of the LORD, for the LORD is about to pass by."
>
> Then a great and powerful wind tore the mountains apart and shattered the rocks before the LORD, but the LORD was not in the wind. After the wind there was an earthquake, but the LORD was not in the earthquake. After the earthquake came a fire, but the LORD was not in the fire. And after the fire came a gentle whisper. (1 Kings 19:11–12)

A gentle whisper. "A still small voice," as some translations have it. To hear that gentle whisper, we have to settle down. Shut out all the drama. Quiet our hearts. Now, as we grow in our personal holiness, we can be quiet and surrendered even in the major questions. But that takes time, and maturity. Don't ask that of yourself as you are starting out. Begin with simple questions. I can sit quietly with the question, *What do you want for this weekend: should we go to the ranch or stay home?* It's not a life-and-death matter. I am not desperately hoping to hear what I secretly want to hear. There is not a great deal of drama around it.

What I'll do is sit with the question before God for several minutes. To help me stay present to God and not begin to wander (*Did I take the socks out of the dryer? Is tomorrow the phone call with my publisher? Where did I leave my cell phone?*), I will repeat the question quietly in my heart. *God, do you want us to go to the ranch or stay home?* I am settling myself before God. *Do you want us to go to the ranch or stay home?* Settle down and be present to God. Pause and listen. Repeat the question. *Should we go to the ranch or stay home? What is your counsel?*

And while I am doing this, I am also noticing my heart's posture on the matter. Am I willing to hear whatever it is God wants to say? That is absolutely critical. If I can only hear an answer that agrees with what I want to hear, then I am not in a posture of surrender to God's will, and it will be hard for me to hear him at all—or to trust what I *do* hear, especially if it is the answer I'm looking for. There is no more decisive issue when it comes to hearing the voice of God than the issue of surrender. Which is beautiful, really. We are drawn to God in search of guidance, but we come away with a deeper holiness because we are learning surrender. Sometimes I will even say as I'm listening, *Lord—I will accept whatever it is you want to say to me.* It helps me bring my soul to a posture of quiet surrender.

So there are the basics: Start with small questions. Repeat the question quietly in your heart to God. Bring yourself to a posture of quiet surrender. And let me add this—I am assuming we are talking about matters of counsel or guidance that are not directly addressed by Scripture. You don't need to ask God whether or not to commit murder or to run off with your neighbor's television. He already spoke to you about those things. You don't need to ask him if you should rest. He spoke to us about that too. But sometimes we don't know where or when or exactly how to rest, and so we need to seek further direction by listening.

Now, if I don't seem to be able to hear God's voice in that moment, sometimes what I will do is "try on" one answer and then the other. Still in a posture of quiet surrender, I ask the Lord, *Is it yes, you want us to go?* Pause. In my heart I am trying it on, letting it be as though this is God's answer. *We should go?* Pause and listen. *Or is it no, you want us to stay home?* Pause and let this be his answer. *We should stay home?* Pause and listen again.

Quite often we can sense God's direction on a matter before we hear actual words. You may have heard someone use the expression "I had a check in my spirit." It refers to an internal pause, a hesitancy, a sudden reluctance to proceed. The Spirit of God may be impressing you with the will of God by making one answer seem very unappealing or wrong somehow. Arresting you, stopping you. Our spirit is in union with the Spirit of God, and he often makes his will known to us deep within before it forms into words. By "trying on" the possible answers, I find it enables me to come into alignment with his Spirit. And, over time, those deep impressions begin to form into words. A simple yes or no can be so encouraging as we learn to listen.

I heard, *Yes—go. It will be good.*

(More at walkingwithgod.net)

Whole and Holy

And now it's raining.

I'm pretty darn sure God told me to come, and now it's raining.

Don't let this throw you. Things may not unfold the way you think they will when you're following God. Remember—he is after both our transformation *and* our joy. The one hangs upon the other. I needed rest more than I knew. But I am so addicted to busyness, I was about to turn his gift of rest into a week of chores. Fix the fence, paint the door, get 'er done. So he has to pin me down on the porch so that I don't wreck the gift he's trying to give.

And now that I am pinned down, I can see what God is bringing to the surface. I am acutely aware of my drivenness. If I keep up this pace, I will burn out. Have a heart attack. Go down in flames. And now I can walk with God even more intimately as I cooperate with him in my transformation. He's got me here on the porch so that he can bring to the surface just how compelled I am. And so that, together, we can explore why. This rain shows no signs of letting up. Looks like we have hours to discover what God is after.

Pause. You *do* know what he is after in your own life, don't you? Maybe that's why we stay so busy—to avoid knowing, so we can avoid dealing with it.

And you do know that the "quick fix" doesn't ever work. Simply telling myself, "You are too busy, John. You've got to slow down," is about as effective as telling an addict to quit. (Has it worked for you?)

There are forces driving the way I live, reasons and compulsions written deep in my soul. I know where my pushing and striving come from. They come from unbelief, from some deep fear that it's all up to me. Life is up to me. I've got to make as much headway as I can before the bottom drops out. Make hay while the sun shines 'cause it isn't always going to shine and what's *that* underlying dread? God is not just after behavior modification (as in, stop it), but real and deep and lasting change.

And that brings me to another assumption that we must hold if we would walk with God—true holiness requires the healing of our souls.

> How blessed is God! And what a blessing he is! He's the Father of our Master, Jesus Christ, and takes us to the high places of blessing in him. Long before he laid down earth's foundations, he had us in mind, had settled on us as the focus of his love, to be made whole and holy by his love. (Ephesians 1:3–4 MSG)

Whole and holy. The two go hand in hand. Oh, how important this is. You can't find the holiness you want without deep wholeness. And you can't find the wholeness you want without deep holiness. You can't simply tell the meth addict to quit. She does *need to* quit, but she requires profound healing *to be able to* quit. You can't just tell a raging man to stop losing his temper. He would love to stop. He'd give anything to stop. He doesn't know how. He doesn't know all the forces within him that swell up and overwhelm him with anger. Telling him to stop raging is like telling him to hold back the sea.

For too long there have been two camps in Christendom. One is the holiness, or "righteousness," crowd. They are the folks holding up the standard, preaching a message of moral purity. The results have been . . . mixed. Some morality, and a great deal of guilt and shame. Very little lasting change comes from this approach. Hey, I'm all for purity. It's just that you can't get there without the healing of your soul.

> God disciplines us for our good, that we may share in his holiness. No discipline seems pleasant at the time, but painful. Later on, however, it produces a harvest of righteousness and peace for those who have been trained by it.
>
> Therefore, strengthen your feeble arms and weak knees. "Make level paths for your feet," so that the lame may not be disabled, but rather healed. (Hebrews 12:10–13)

Healed. As in fixed. Restored. Made whole. The Bible says we can't hope to walk the path God would have us walk without the healing of our souls. Now, the other major camp is the "grace" camp. Their message is that we can't hope to satisfy a holy God, but we are forgiven. We are under grace. And praise the living God, we are under grace. But what about holiness? What about deep personal change? Paul says, "For sin shall not be your master, because you are not under law, but under grace" (Romans 6:14). He's assuming that a certain kind of grace will set us free from sin's power over our daily lives.

My drivenness and compulsion will ruin me if they continue. God knows that. He also knows what I need. Sitting here on the porch, I am asking him to come into the deep places of my soul and heal me. I know, at least in part, what my drivenness is rooted in. Early on in my life, I found myself alone. It was a deep and profound wounding. No boy is meant to be on his own. But that wounding led to a sinful resolution—*I will make it on my own.* I felt that life was up to me (that was my wounding). I resolved to live as though life were up to me (that was my sin). The path to freedom from all this pushing and striving involves *both* repentance and healing so that I can be made whole and holy by his love. Listen to Jesus:

> "'For this people's heart has become calloused;
>> they hardly hear with their ears,
>> and they have closed their eyes.
> Otherwise they might see with their eyes,
>> hear with their ears,
>> understand with their hearts
> and turn, and I would heal them.'" (Matthew 13:15)

Heal them. Jesus yearned for his people to turn back to him *so that* he could heal them! The "otherwise" means that if they weren't so hardheaded, they would turn to him and he would heal them. This truth is essential to your view of the gospel. It will shape your convictions about nearly everything else. God wants to restore us. Our part is to "turn," to repent as best we can. But we also need his healing. As Ephesians 1:4 says, God chose us to make us whole and holy through his love. God will make known to us the path of life if we will follow him. And as we do, we will find along that path our need for wholeness and holiness.

And so I'm praying, and journaling:

> *Jesus, forgive me. I ask your forgiveness of this deep commitment to make life work on my own—for all my striving and pushing and for all the unbelief that propels me. Forgive me.*
>
> *And I ask you to heal me of this. Heal the places in my soul that have so long felt alone, felt that life was up to me.*

And as I'm praying this, I remember something God has been saying to me for some time. Or rather, he speaks it to me again. It addresses the deep fears in my heart, speaks to the core of this issue.

My favor will never leave you.

And a soft, cool breeze caresses my face.

Making Room for Joy

A few years ago a woman with a sensitive spirit and a keen eye for what God is up to pulled me aside to offer this warning: "The battle in your life is against your joy."

It hit me like a Mack truck.

But of course. Suddenly life made sense. The hassles. The battles. The disappointments. The losses. The resignation. Why hadn't I seen it before? I mean, I face a lot of different skirmishes day to day, but now the plot, the diabolical plot behind them all came into view. I began to see how the enemy was first trying to take away all joy from my life. Wear me down. Then, weary and thirsty, I would be quite vulnerable to some counterfeit joy. It would start with mild addictions, then build to something worse. Thus he would destroy all that God has done in and through me. It was so obvious. Of course.

Her observation became a revelation became a rescue. The smoke alarm sounding off before the house goes up in flames. For several days the whole world made sense in light of joy. But in the day-to-day grind of the ensuing months, all that clarity slipped away. Completely. Joy as a category seemed . . . irrelevant. Nice but unessential. Like owning a hot tub. And distant too. The hot tub is in Fiji. Wouldn't it be nice? Ain't going to happen. Life's not really about joy. I've got all this *stuff* that has to get done. The mail is stacking up, and I haven't paid the bills in two months. The Service Engine Soon light came on in the Honda. Joy? Life's about surviving—and getting a little pleasure. That's what seemed true.

Really now—how much do you think about joy? Do you see it as essential to your life, something God insists on?

Yesterday morning my sons Sam, Blaine, and I rode our horses together up through the woods. The sunlight was filtering down through the aspens as we followed an old game trail we'd never taken before. Our golden retriever, Scout, was running on ahead of us. The horses seemed to be enjoying the ride as much as we were. It was cool under the canopy of aspens. Quiet. Timeless. In the evening Blaine and I took the canoe over to a high mountain reservoir fed by a beautiful rushing stream. We paddled about a half mile from the put-in back to the inlet. The trout were rising. Not another soul was around. For an hour we caught rainbows on dry flies, surrounded by mountains, the rushing inlet the only sound of the evening. On the way home we saw a fox, and a porcupine.

It was an incredible day. One of those rare and glorious days that become, over time, the icon of summer vacation in our memories.

So, why don't I wake with a joyful heart today? Joy was just here. Where did it go?

I feel like I met a stranger on an airplane, and we clicked. We swapped some stories, had a few drinks, laughed together. Then I drove home to an empty house. It's like that. I had an encounter with joy. It touched a longing. Now I begin to realize I haven't even given ten minutes to joy, let alone pursued it as essential to my life.

It has to do with agreements I've made without even knowing it. By "agreements" I mean those subtle convictions we come to, assent to, give way to, or are raised to assume are true. It happens down deep in our souls where our real beliefs about life are formed. Something or someone whispers to us, *Life is never going to turn out the way you'd hoped*, or *Nobody's going to come through*, or *God has forsaken you*. And something in us responds, *That's true*. We make an agreement with it, and a conviction is formed. It seems so reasonable. I think we come to more of our beliefs in this way than maybe any other. Subtle agreements.

Anyhow, I began to realize that what I've done for most of my life is resign myself to this idea: *I'm really not going to have any lasting joy*. And from that resignation, I've gone on to try and find what I could have. Women do this in marriage. They see that they are not going to have any real intimacy with their husbands, so they lose themselves in soaps or tabloids or romance novels. Men find their work a sort of slow death, so they get a little something in the bar scene each night. Have a few beers with the boys, watch the game. Joy isn't even a consideration. Settle for relief.

Now, to be fair, joy isn't exactly falling from the sky these days. We don't go out to gather it each morning like manna. It's hard to come by. Joy seems more elusive than winning the lottery. We don't like to think about it much, because it hurts to allow ourselves to feel how much we long for joy, and how seldom it drops by.

But joy *is* the point. I know it is. God says that joy is our strength. "The joy of the LORD is your strength" (Nehemiah 8:10). I think, *My strength? I don't even think of it as my occasional boost.* But yes, now that I give it some thought, I can see that when I have felt joy I have felt more alive than at any other time in my life. Pull up a memory of one of your best moments. The day at the beach. Your eighth birthday. Remember how you felt. Now think what life would be like if you felt like that on a regular basis. Maybe that's what being strengthened by joy feels like. It would be good.

I take up a concordance and begin to read a bit on joy.

"My heart leaps for joy" (Psalm 28:7). When was the last time my heart leapt for joy? I don't even remember.

"You have filled my heart with greater joy than when their grain and new wine abound" (Psalm 4:7). I believe David when he says this. I believe God does this. I just can't say I really know firsthand what he's talking about.

I turn to the Gospels. What does Jesus have to say about joy?

"I have told you this so that my joy may be in you and that your joy may be complete." (John 15:11)

"Until now you have not asked for anything in my name. Ask and you will receive, and your joy will be complete." (John 16:24)

"I am coming to you now, but I say these things while I am still in the world, so that they may have the full measure of my joy within them." (John 17:13)

Joy complete? The full measure of his joy? That's what Jesus wants for us? I'm almost stunned. I can't believe that it's come down to joy. It's so obvious now, yet it makes me really uncomfortable. Probably because it's too close to my heart, to what I long for. Joy is such a tender thing, I think we resent it. We avoid it, because it feels too vulnerable to allow ourselves to admit the joy we long for but do not have.

Jesus, I have no idea where to go from here. But I invite you in. Take me where I need to go. I know this is connected to the life you want me to live.

What Should I Read?

Let's come back to the place of the Bible in our walk with God.

God speaks to us through the Bible. And what is said there has more authority than anything else in our lives. It is the bedrock of our faith, the test of all things, a living connection to the heart and mind of God—when we approach it with the help of the Spirit of God. I add that qualifier because we do well to remember that the Pharisees read and studied the Bible, "but their minds were made dull, for to this day the same veil remains when the old covenant is read. It has not been removed, because only in Christ is it taken away. Even to this day when Moses is read, a veil covers their hearts" (2 Corinthians 3:14–15). How very sad. They read it, but they didn't get it.

The Bible is not a magic book. It doesn't reveal its treasures simply because you read a passage. It doesn't make you holy simply because you hold it in high esteem. Many cults use the Bible. Even Satan quotes Scripture (see Luke 4:9–12). We need the Bible and all it has to say to us. Desperately. We also need the Spirit of God to guide us in our reading and study. "All this I have spoken while still with you," Jesus said, as he was preparing his followers for life after his departure. "But the Counselor, the Holy Spirit, whom the Father will send in my name, will teach you all things and will remind you of everything I have said to you" (John 14:25–26).

We need God to help us understand his Word. We can't separate a walk with God from our reading of Scripture. The two go hand in hand. Like having a tour guide as you wander the halls of the Louvre. "If you love me, you will obey what I command. And I will ask the Father, and he will give you another Counselor to be with you forever—the Spirit of truth. The world cannot accept him, because it neither sees him nor knows him. But you know him, for he lives with you and will be in you" (John 14:15–17). Too many people approach Scripture without an intimacy with God, and they either end up frustrated because they've gotten so little out of it or, far worse, amass an intellectual understanding quite apart from any real communion with God. It usually results in religious pride.

The Bible is meant to be read in fellowship with God. Things can get really weird if we don't.

Having offered that caveat, let me say that the more we know the Scriptures and, the more they become a part of us, the more we'll find that we *can* walk with God. Having spent a good deal of time in the Word of God, you'll give the Holy Spirit a library within you to draw upon. For example, I'll be sitting in a meeting and getting mad, and the Spirit reminds me, "Man's anger does not bring about the righteous life that God desires" (James 1:20). I cool down. Or I'll walk by the tabloids in the bookstore, sirens on every cover, and the Spirit reminds me, "Do not lust in your heart after her beauty" (Proverbs 6:25). Or I'll see a gorgeous vista in the mountains, and because I know "the earth is the LORD's, and everything in it" (Psalm 24:1), my heart fills with gratitude and I'll be reminded of what God is like through his creation.

There is no substitute for the written Word of God. No matter how precious a personal word may be to us, no matter how cool some insight may be, it doesn't compare to the written Word. I've seen too many immature Christians chase after "revelation" and go wacky because they are not rooted and grounded in the Scripture.

> The precepts of the LORD are right,
>> giving joy to the heart.
> The commands of the LORD are radiant,
>> giving light to the eyes.
> The fear of the LORD is pure,
>> enduring forever.
> The ordinances of the LORD are sure
>> and altogether righteous.
> They are more precious than gold,
>> than much pure gold;
> they are sweeter than honey,
>> than honey from the comb.
> By them is your servant warned;
>> in keeping them there is great reward.
> (Psalm 19:8–11)

But *what* to read?

It's a big book, even with the microprint on tissue paper. There's a lot to take in. All sorts of different content and styles. It can feel like picking up *War and Peace* or Robertson's biography of Stonewall Jackson. Now, I'm all for the various programs available to help us read through the Bible in a year or study a certain book. It helps so much to know context and history. Commentaries, concordances, and electronic Bible study software abound—I use them all and benefit from them.

But in addition to all that, let me add how rich it can be simply to ask God, *What would you have me read today?*

Letting your Shepherd lead you in your reading allows him to take you right to a passage that you may not have thought of yourself or that may not have been in line with the recent program you were using, but is the *very* word you need. In this way I have received many warnings, endless counsel, immeasurable comfort, and the incomparable intimacy of God speaking directly to me through his Word.

Just this morning I asked God what to read. At first I simply heard, *John.* So I open my Bible to the gospel of John, and as I turn there I ask, *Where in John?* and God says, *Ten.* (He's said this several times these past few mornings.) Now, I realize that hearing God in such a direct manner might be a new experience for you. It certainly wasn't my experience for years. No shame in that. We're students, and we're all learning. Don't let your experience of God up to this point limit what you might enjoy with him in the coming years.

I began to read in John 10, not really knowing yet what God was up to, but expectant. I knew that even if I didn't discern exactly why I was in this passage this morning, I know I would benefit from being here. So I was good either way. This is what I read:

> "I tell you the truth, the man who does not enter the sheep pen by the gate, but climbs in by some other way, is a thief and a robber. The man who enters by the gate is the shepherd of his sheep. The watchman opens the gate for him, and the sheep listen to his voice. He calls his own sheep by name and leads them out. When he has brought out all his own, he goes on ahead of them, and his sheep follow him because they know his voice." (John 10:1–4)

I love this passage and have spent a good deal of time here. But today I'm struck by the phrase "he goes on ahead of them." It's almost as if I'd never noticed it before, never given it my heart's attention. Jesus goes ahead of us. That is so reassuring, and that is *such* a different view than the one with which I approach each day. Or better, it reveals to me the way that I see each day. Here's what happens.

I connect with God in the morning in prayer and sometimes through reading of some sort. But then a shift occurs. Somewhere between prayer, and having breakfast, and getting the boys off to school, and getting to work myself, and beginning to answer e-mails and tackle projects, a subtle parting occurs. I don't feel as though I am following Jesus going ahead of me. I just sort of take it for granted that I am blazing the trail. Until this morning I never would have put it into those words. But this passage makes me realize that I don't see our relationship as God going on ahead of me. But I want to. Oh, how I want to. My heart is engaged. This is no intellectual exercise, but a living and immediate conversation with God through his Word.

Do you really, Jesus? Do you really go on ahead of me?

That is such a better view of God, a view where he is engaged with us and intimately involved in the world and in our lives. As I think about it now, I think I have been something of an unconscious Deist. God is there, but I'm doing my darnedest down here while he is sort of smiling down on me, not really engaged in the details. That view is not true of him, and it is an awful way to live. I think of George MacDonald's wonderful insight:

If to myself—"God sometimes interferes"—
I said, my faith at once would be struck blind.

I see him all in all . . .
A love he is that watches and that hears
(*Diary of an Old Soul*)

I do believe this. Why don't I believe it in the day-to-day events of my life? Maybe the issue goes more like this: I do believe Christ leads us, but I make no *conscious* effort to follow him in all the "in-between" times, where life is really being lived. The question is, will I follow God, as opposed to just going on my way into each day? That is the transition to a better life. To be asking him where he is headed and what he is doing throughout the day. So that while he *is* going on ahead of me, I am following.

This was just what I needed to read this morning, just what the doctor ordered.

Now, there are other times when I'll read what I think God has prompted me to read, and at the time it doesn't make any sense at all. Several weeks ago it was *John 7*. I read the whole chapter, and while I appreciated the story, it was flat. Like reading the periodic table of elements. I sort of shrugged my shoulders and went into the day, knowing that whatever God meant by the passage, if I even heard him right, he would bring it around. A few days went by, and I was driving down the road one day thinking about how tied up in knots I get when I'm self-conscious about what others think of me.

Then it was as if the Spirit brought me back to John 7.

Among the crowds there was widespread whispering about him. Some said, "He is a good man."

Others replied, "No, he deceives the people." But no one would say anything publicly about him for fear of the Jews.

Not until halfway through the Feast did Jesus go up to the temple courts and begin to teach. The Jews were amazed and asked, "How did this man get such learning without having studied?"

Jesus answered, "My teaching is not my own. It comes from him who sent me. If anyone chooses to do God's will, he will find out whether my teaching comes from God or whether I speak on my own. He who speaks on his own does so to gain honor for himself, but he who works for the honor of the one who sent him is a man of truth; there is nothing false about him." (vv. 12–18)

There is such a freedom in Jesus. He didn't care what the religious scholars thought about him, good or bad. He didn't let the current of public opinion sway him either way. He just said what he had to say, knowing he was approved by his Father.

Oh, this is what you were pointing to. This is what you wanted me to see.

Yes.

Lord, I want the freedom you have. To be completely free of what others think of me.

Give it a try. Ask God what he would have you read. Settle yourself, quiet your heart. Let go of the pressure that says you *have* to hear from him right now or things aren't right between you. Things are fine. You are his. Rest your heart and your relationship there. Then ask this simple question: *God, what would you have me read today?* Pause and listen. Repeat the question. If you begin to get an impression, or believe you heard him say something, repeat it. *Was that John 10, Lord? You want me to read John 10?* (That "trying it on" thing.) Practice this over the course of several weeks.

You will be delighted with what unfolds.

When We Don't Hear God

I cannot find my watch this morning. And it's driving me nuts.

Here I am, with a few precious hours to write, but I keep getting up every fifteen minutes or so to look for my watch. And I can't find it. I don't really need it right now. I don't have to be anywhere for another hour and a half. But I think it's the idea that I *can't* find it that's got me obsessed *with* finding it. I just took another lap around the house, looking in all the usual places—the nightstand, the bathroom counter, behind the cushions on the sofa—and it isn't there. (It wasn't there when I rooted around fifteen minutes ago either. Do I think it's going to magically appear?) Then it occurs to me, *You* are *writing a book on walking with God. Why don't you ask him where it is?*

Okay. So I pray, "God, you know where my watch is. Where is it?"

Silence. I don't hear anything.

I don't know why. But I'm not going to let that be the verdict on my relationship with God today. This is really important, friends. We don't know on any given day all that's playing into why we can't seem to hear from God. It could be that I'm still too distracted, obsessed with finding my watch myself. It could be that the enemy is blocking me. It could be that God isn't going to speak on this right now. It could be that he wants me to discover something else—like why I am so obsessed with finding my watch when I don't need it and I really should be writing. I don't know all that's going on.

But I do know this: it can't be the verdict of how I'm doing with God or how he feels about me in this moment.

Hearing from God *flows out of* our relationship. That relationship was established for us by Jesus Christ. "Therefore, since we have been justified [made right with God] through faith, we have peace with God through our Lord Jesus Christ, through whom we have gained access by faith into this grace in which we now stand" (Romans 5:1). Whatever we might be feeling, we do have relationship with God now, because we belong to him. And our relationship is secure. "I am convinced that neither death nor life, neither angels nor demons, neither the present nor the future, nor any powers, neither height nor depth, nor anything else in all creation, will be able to separate us from the love of God that is in Christ Jesus our Lord" (Romans 8:38–39).

I am God's. He is mine.

Because we *do* have relationship with God secured for us by Jesus Christ and all he has done, we can now grow in *developing* that relationship. We can, on the basis of what is objectively true, move into an experience of God in our lives that deepens over time. And that includes learning to hear his voice. Prayer not as making speeches to God, a one-sided conversation, but as the act of talking to and hearing from God. A two-sided conversation. It is a rich inheritance we have.

My ability to hear God's voice on any given day does not change my position in Christ one bit. I share this because the last thing I want to introduce into your faith is shame or doubt or some other attack because you're not hearing clearly right now. Taking the journey toward an intimacy with God that includes conversational intimacy is a beautiful thing, full of surprises and gifts from him.

But it can also send us reeling if we are basing our relationship with God on our ability to hear from him in this moment or on this particular issue. I know that's happened to me. Our faith is based on something much more solid than today's episode. We have the Scriptures, given to us by God, and they are the bedrock for everything else. They tell us that because we have placed our faith in God, we belong to him and are completely secure. They tell us that he is involved in our lives today, whether we feel it or not. They tell us he will never, ever abandon us.

So, if you're not yet hearing, don't worry. It's okay. Keep praying. Keep listening. Notice what God might be up to other than answering the immediate question. Like right now, what I notice is that I want to start blaming people. *Who stole my watch? I'll bet it was Stasi.* Geez, Louise, what is *that*? Why am I so quick to find someone to blame? I'm laughing at myself. *Easy there, buddy. You don't know that. Don't go jumping to a federal indictment here.* What I need to do right now is just let it go. Let it go.

This story has a playful ending.

An hour and a half has gone by, now it's time for me to leave, and I really would love to have my watch. So I pray again, *Jesus, help me find my watch.* I'm not pushing into hearing right now; I'm trusting something deeper—that he's here and that he can guide me in other ways. This isn't an all-or-nothing proposition. It's not either I hear from God or he isn't involved. Not at all. I go into the bedroom, grab a pair of socks out of the drawer, and sit down in the middle of the floor to put them on. I don't think I've ever done this before, sat down in this particular spot to put on my socks. But from this angle I can see under the bed. And there it is. My watch.

I sense God smiling.

You Shall Know Them by Their Fruit

I'm trying to write this morning, but I can't seem to concentrate. I just can't seem to find the groove.

Over the past twenty minutes, I've tried several approaches to dealing with this. I've laid out an outline to help me think clearly. I've gone to a different section of the book to see if I might be more inspired there. I've given in to distraction—checking my e-mail, wandering around the house, hoping that when I return I'll be my old self again. Nothing seems to be working. And now it dawns on me—who would have a vested interest in thwarting the progress of this book? Who would be delighted to distract me for a month, let alone a day? Who would want to distort my thinking just enough to diminish the beauty or the helpfulness of what I'm trying to say?

You shall know them, Jesus said, by their fruit.

The principle holds true for anything in life. It is especially helpful in diagnosing what the enemy might be up to. What is the fruit of what you're experiencing? What is its *effect*? If it continues, what will the results of that be? What will be lost? Jesus said he came that we might have life and have it abundantly. He also warned that the thief comes to steal, kill, and destroy. Is something being stolen? That's not from God. He called Satan the accuser of the brethren. Are you under accusation, that feeling of "I'm such an idiot"? (I'm using polite language here.) Look at the fruit—it will give you a good idea of the tree it came from.

Paul says that "the fruit of the Spirit is love, joy, peace, patience, kindness, goodness, faithfulness, gentleness and self-control" (Galatians 5:22). I'm not feeling real joyful at the moment. In fact, the longer whatever this oppression is hangs around, the more discouraged I get. There's not a lot of peace here either. Not like a river. Not even a rivulet. Whatever this cloud is I'm under, it isn't bringing with it the fruit of the Spirit. I can't get back to the clear air I normally have when I'm writing. Something is in the way.

It's vague, I can't quite name it yet, but I sure can see the fruit of it. I can't write.

Now, certainly, we need to beware the fruit of the flesh. Paul names those as "sexual immorality, impurity and debauchery; idolatry and witchcraft; hatred, discord, jealousy, fits of rage, selfish ambition, dissensions, factions and envy; drunkenness, orgies, and the like" (Galatians 5:19). Nope. None of that seems to be going on here. I'm certainly open to conviction of sin, but I'm not raging, and I'm not drunk. And it's not like writer's block is in the list. Something else is in the way.

The first major awakening in our journey of faith is coming to realize that God exists. It can be quite a jolt. The second, and far more life-changing, epiphany is when we come to realize that we have to deal with him. Take him into account. We come to see that God is not to be ignored. This is an even bigger jolt and a major course correction for any human being. Many people avoid it for years. But hopefully, we come to see that there is no better way than to place our love and trust in God, accept his invitation to life, and give our hearts to him. We become his sons and daughters through faith in Jesus Christ. And hopefully his followers.

But there is another major awakening. The next epiphany in our journey of faith is coming to realize that Satan exists. And that we have to deal with him too. We come to realize that he is not to be ignored either. I'm sorry to say that this awakening is uncommon, even among the followers of Christ—despite the fact that Scripture is filled with warnings of an enemy.

And there was war in heaven. Michael and his angels fought against the dragon, and the dragon and his angels fought back.

But he was not strong enough, and they lost their place in heaven. The great dragon was hurled down—that ancient serpent called the devil, or Satan, who leads the whole world astray. He was hurled to the earth, and his angels with him. . . . Then the dragon was enraged . . . and went off to make war against . . . those who obey God's commandments and hold to the testimony of Jesus. (Revelation 12:7–9, 17)

Satan has been hurled to the earth. Along with all his forces of fallen angels. (They're called demons.) They are making war now against those who have become the friends of God. Except most of the friends of God don't know it. I didn't know it for years. I was ignorant. In the dark. But this is a very helpful thing to know. It will shed a great deal of light on the events of your life.

Let's come back to the naive assumption that A + B = C. Be good. Believe in God. And all will be well. *No*, Jesus said. *There is more going on here. You have an enemy. You have to take that into account, or you won't find the life I am offering you.* Judging by the fruit of my discouragement and lack of clarity, and the fact that God seems far away this morning, I've got a pretty good hunch that the enemy is here, jamming my writing process.

So I have to stop and pray.

Do It Now

I have to pray about this *now*.

But whenever I'm facing spiritual attack of any kind, the pull is nearly always to try and ignore it, push it off till later, or explain it away as bad digestion or my ongoing inadequacies or something else. Anything else. I see this in all my friends as well. We just don't want to deal with it.

God gave us a will. Learning to exercise it is a great part of maturing as a person. You don't want to get out of bed in the morning? You'll lose your job. You don't want to deny yourself anything? You'll go into debt. This is Growing Up 101. And there is nothing like spiritual warfare to teach you to exercise your will. For one thing, you won't want to deal with it. So the best thing you can do is turn, face the attack, and deal with it. Now. It strengthens your will. But most Christians end up not really praying directly against the attack. They'll pray something like *Jesus, I ask you to take this away.* If it's discouragement they're dealing with, they may pray, *I ask you to encourage me.* And it's a good thing to be encouraged. Or let's say it's lust they've been confronted with. Most folks will then pray, *Give me pure thoughts, Lord.* And it's a good thing to ask for pure thoughts.

But they are still dodging the issue.

The enemy is present in the form of some foul spirit, and *you* must command him to leave. As the Scripture urges, "Resist the devil, and he will flee from you" (James 4:7). No resist, no flee. We are *commanded* to resist. Paul shows us how it's done. "Finally Paul became so troubled that he turned around and said to the spirit, 'In the name of Jesus Christ I command you to come out of her!' At that moment the spirit left her" (Acts 16:18). Out loud. In the name of Jesus Christ. That's how it's done.

Now, it really helps if you can name the spirit. You are dealing with a distorted being here, a foul spirit filled with disobedience and deception. It may duck and maneuver and refuse to leave. You've got to be direct, and you have to be authoritative. "'Be quiet!' Jesus said sternly" (Luke 4:35). Note the word *sternly*.

Sometimes you know what you are dealing with by its fruit. You're suddenly slammed with lust—then it's Lust you must banish. You're under a malaise of despair—then it's Despair you must banish. But even better at this point is to *stop and ask God* what you're dealing with. Don't just swing wildly away at it. Ask Jesus what you need to pray against. As you grow in your ability to hear God's voice, this will become very helpful in dealing with the enemy. Quite often now, after years of practice, I'll just start praying, and as I'm praying I listen to the Lord and pray what he tells me to pray. Here is how I prayed this morning:

"I bring the kingdom of God, the glory of the Lord Jesus Christ, and the fullness of the work of Christ against this spirit of distraction and against all foul spirits here." Distraction doesn't quite seem to hit the mark, so I ask God, *What is it, Lord—what am I dealing with here?*

Diminishment, he says. Oh yes, that's been an enemy of mine for many years. A spirit of Diminishment. Okay. "I bring the full work of the Lord Jesus Christ against Diminishment, and I bind Diminishment from me." Remember, Jesus says to "tie up the strong man" (Matthew 12:29). Clearly the context of his instruction is dealing with foul spirits, because in the preceding verse he has just said, "But if I drive out demons by the Spirit of God, then the kingdom of God has come upon you" (v. 28). Then he says to bind the enemy.

Next I pause for a moment and ask Christ, *Is there anything else I need to pray?*

Cleanse yourself with my blood and ask my Spirit to restore you in me, restore our union, and inspire you.

"I cleanse myself with the blood of the Lord Jesus Christ. I bring the blood of Jesus over my spirit, soul, and body, over my heart, mind, and will. I ask your Spirit, Jesus, to restore me in you, renew me in you, to renew our union, and to inspire me. In the name of Jesus."

There, I'm already feeling better. Not completely better— sometimes these things take a bit of time to be worked out in the spiritual realm. But I'm better now, and I'm going to keep an eye out for any further assault. If I'm not completely better in thirty minutes or so—meaning clear and no longer "under it"—then I'll stop and pray like this again.

Now, I know this can sound kind of weird or spooky. But the Scriptures make it very plain that the followers of Christ will experience spiritual attack. "Be self-controlled and alert. Your enemy the devil prowls around like a roaring lion looking for someone to devour. Resist him, standing firm in the faith, because you know that your brothers throughout the world are undergoing the same kind of sufferings" (1 Peter 5:8–9). "Your brothers" means fellow Christians. And "throughout the world" means that these spiritual attacks aren't just limited to a Billy Graham crusade or a mission to New Guinea. They are part of the Christian life.

I suppose I pray against some form of assault every other day or so. When things are bad, every day. You might think that's a lot, but you'll soon discover that if you want life and joy, if you are moving into deeper intimacy with God, you are going to attract attention. The enemy will not like it. That's okay. Don't surrender. Don't back down. As Scripture says, resist. Rise up. Fight back. If you do, you can be rid of the attack. And best of all, it makes you holy. Because it strengthens your will and draws you closer to Christ. It causes you to mature, for you have to be intentional and deal with assaults directly.

No more dodging.

(More at walkingwithgod.net)

Beware of Agreements

How much of this oppressive stuff do we live under and how much joy do we surrender because we never stop to ask, "Where is this crud coming from?" I could have assumed that I was just having an off morning. I could have chalked up the distractions to writer's block. It would have been so easy to do so, so very easy to make a subtle agreement, something along the lines of, *I guess I'm just not going to get anything done today.* You have to be really careful about these agreements.

We know the enemy is a liar. In fact, he's the father of all lies (John 8:44). We also know he is cunning. More cunning than any creature God created (Genesis 3:1). So, we might expect him to be rather good at getting us to believe his lies. Very, very good. His attacks are often quite subtle, masquerading as something else (like writer's block). What he's hoping is that we won't see an attack for what it is, and that we'll go ahead and make an agreement with it. Let me show you how this works.

We were catching up with some old friends over dinner one night, a couple we hadn't seen in years. During the course of the evening, we talked about our kids and what they were up to and about trips we'd been on. A wonderful free-roaming conversation. Suddenly the woman (I'll call her Anne) stopped me midstory. "You guys keep saying things like 'Then God told us to' or 'We asked God, and he said. . . .' You act like God speaks to you all the time."

"Well, no, not all the time," I said. "But often, yes."

She had a troubled look on her face. "I've never heard the voice of God." Now, mind you, this dear woman loves God and has been a Christian for thirty years, a pastor's wife for much of that time.

"What if that's not you, Anne?" I said. "I mean, what if that's not because of you?" Tears began to well up in her eyes. She thought it was her fault. We all do that. We think it's us. "Who would have a vested interest in you not hearing the voice of God?"

"Satan, I guess," she said halfheartedly. She wasn't a big believer in spiritual warfare. "Let's do this—let's pray and see if there is anything in the way, anything that might be blocking you from hearing God's voice." The four of us got up from the table, went into the living room, sat down, and began to pray, asking, "Jesus, is anything in the way of Anne hearing from you?" We sit for several minutes in silence. I can tell that we're butting up against something, partly because I'm suddenly hit with an overwhelming sense of *This isn't going to work. You shouldn't be doing this.*

Then Stasi said, "Well, I hear the word *abandonment.*"

Okay. Abandonment. You never know where these things are going to take you. I turned back to Anne and asked, "Have you ever felt abandoned, Anne?" More tears. She can't speak but just nods. "Tell us."

She began to recount a story from early on in her Christian life. Her first baby had terrible colic and screamed all day. He was a royal screamer. She reached her breaking point one day and cried out in desperation for God to make him stop. But he didn't. The enemy was there in a moment. *You see, God has abandoned you,* he said. And something in her heart agreed. She made an agreement. *God has abandoned me.* And a curtain fell in Anne's heart between her and God.

Paul warns us that unresolved emotional issues can create spiritual strongholds in a Christian's life. "'In your anger do not sin.' Do not let the sun go down while you are still angry, and do not give the devil a foothold" (Ephesians 4:26–27). Paul was writing a letter to believers, and he is pretty clear here that the ways we mishandle the events of our lives can give the enemy a foothold or stronghold in our lives. Again, there's nothing weird or spooky here, just part of the battle and something we have to deal with. The fruit is that Anne can't hear from God. That's certainly not the fruit of the Spirit.

"Jesus, how do we pray about this?" I asked. *Have her break the agreement.* So we led Anne in a prayer like this: "Jesus, you promised never to leave me nor forsake me. Forgive me for making the agreement that you abandoned me. I renounce that agreement now. In your name." Having done that, we could then bring the work of Jesus Christ against the spirit of abandonment and against every lying spirit that had brought this to Anne.

Now what? I asked in my heart. *Invite my healing.* So I led Anne in a prayer something like this: "Jesus, I felt so abandoned by you. Come and heal my heart in this place. Come into this memory, this time in my life. Come and minister to me here." We let there be a few moments of silence, let Christ minister to her.

Now what? I asked Christ in my heart. *Ask her if she hears my voice.*

If you've ever driven at night in winter conditions, you know that feeling when you need to hit your brakes and you're hoping you aren't at that moment on a sheet of black ice. That hold-your-breath moment when everything in you says, *I hope this works.* That's how I felt. *Lord, the things you ask me to do.* Whenever we are praying with someone like this, I am very careful not to bring further distress or give the enemy an opportunity by inviting the person to a place he or she might not be ready or able to go. But God said to do it, and so I said, "Anne, Jesus wants you to listen for him now. Would you like to do that?"

She nodded, and we prayed, "Lord Jesus, what do you want to say to your beloved? What is your word to Anne tonight?"

I'm thinking, *You'd better come through.* A long silence. I sneaked a peek at Anne, and she was crying. "What do you hear?"

"He said he loves me."

That was the first time in thirty years she'd heard God speak to her. All because of an agreement.

Being Willing to Have a Look

So, I drive this old '78 Toyota Land Cruiser, and for the most part, I love it. It's a simple, straightforward, no-nonsense truck. No onboard computers, no electric windows, no navigation system. (The last thing I need is a woman's voice telling me where to turn: "Merge right. Exit right in one-quarter mile. Exit now.") I love the simplicity of old cars. Anyhow, I went to move it yesterday evening, but the battery was dead. There's a quirk in the brake lights that makes them stay on sometimes after I've turned off the car, and if I don't pay attention, it drains the battery overnight. Quirkiness comes with old cars. And people.

I solved the problem for the moment by jumping the truck with our other car, but I knew I hadn't driven it far enough or long enough to charge the battery off the alternator, knew I'd have to deal with it this morning before I headed into work. When we jumped it last night, I noticed my battery terminals looked corroded. I thought, *Maybe all I'll need to do is clean them off.* Hope springs eternal.

As I unlatched the hood and propped it open, I was struck by the fact that it's been a long time since I've looked under the hood. I had that nagging feeling, *It's been a long time since you looked at anything under here.* It's not a good feeling, that feeling of neglect and what might need to be faced here. I have the same awkward moment every time I see the floss in the bathroom drawer. Anyhow, back to the Land Cruiser.

The first thing you meet when you look under the hood of most cars is the radiator—the black boxy-looking thing with the little silver cap on top. Water and antifreeze go in there. It's how your car cools itself. I thought, *Uh-oh—when was the last time I checked the water level?* I couldn't even remember. Last summer? Popping the cap off, I see no fluid. *Yikes. Better fill that.* I look around the garage and find an old jug of Prestone and begin to pour it in. The reservoir of the radiator is a labyrinth of tubes, and you never know how much fluid you need in these old cars until you start pouring it in. The more it takes, the longer it has been since you took care of it. Quite a bit goes in before the green stuff finally appears near the top.

As I screw the cap back on, my thoughts turn to the oil. A deeper angst creeps over me. *When was the last time I checked the oil?* I couldn't remember that either. A sort of discomfort-becoming-dread fills my stomach like ice water. It's one thing to forget to keep your radiator filled. If things go wrong, you'll typically find out right away, because your car overheats and steam comes blowing out. But by the time you realize you blew it with your oil, deeper damage has usually been done to your engine. Like a faithful old camel, this Land Cruiser will run till it drops. But you don't want to do that to a car. You don't want to find out you forgot to add oil by having your engine seize.

Now, I'm standing there knowing all this, knowing that I need to check the oil *now*, but something in me hesitated.

I didn't want to know.

I didn't want to go there.

I knew it had been a long time. And I wasn't sure I really wanted the information lying at the end of my dipstick.

Standing there looking down into the front end of my car like an idiot, immobile, I was struck by the fact that I didn't really want to have a look, and I recognized the feeling. I have it around my checkbook. *(When was the last time I balanced it?)* I have it when I drive past the dentist. *(When was my last checkup?)* I have this sinking feeling around anything I know I've neglected, especially if the neglect has carried on for some time.

We do this with our internal life most of all. Something will come up to cause us to realize it has been a long time (have we ever, really?) since we had a look under the hood. An argument with our spouse. A sudden and very strong pull to someone else's spouse. Fear over a coming presentation. Anxiety. Depression. Someone simply asking, "How are you doing?" We sense rumblings beneath the surface, and we don't want to go there.

I had to have a look. This couldn't go on. So I search around to find the dipstick, pull it out with dread, and sigh with relief to see that, though my oil is low, it is not dangerously low. I sigh when I discover I haven't been driving without oil for who knows how long, and the pool of ice water drains out of my stomach. I find a quart of 5W30 on the shelf behind the snow boots and paint cans and pour it in. Then I set about dealing with the battery.

But I had been confronted with this part of me that is part

coward, part hedonist, part magical thinker. This part of me that just doesn't want to be disturbed, not even when the information will save me later on. I see the same thing in all of my friends. I mean, this is universal. We don't want to have a look under the hood. We don't want to know what we desperately need to know. This is not a good quality. It is *not* our friend.

Over the years I've learned a simple lesson: pay now or pay more later. It's true in every area of life. I don't want to exercise, don't want to pay the price. I just want to coast along. But I end up paying for it later when we're out on a hike or swimming in a lake or I'm dashing from Terminal A to Terminal B to try and catch a flight and I'm sucking air and my side is cramping. I know I'll pay even more down the road in terms of my health. I don't want to "pay" in any sense of delayed gratification, don't want to forgo the purchase of something I desire. So I pay nearly twice the amount for the dinner or the iPod or whatever it is by putting it on my credit card and making interest payments over time.

I do it in relationship. I don't want to ask Stasi how things are going, don't want the discomfort of what she might have to say. I don't want to give up the book I'm reading. I mean, this could take hours. So I put off asking until it becomes a major issue. I don't want to step into muddy waters with a friend, tell him what I see—that he is hard to be around—or ask him what's troubling him. So I pay more later when we've grown really distant or I even lose the friendship altogether because the distance is just too far to cross.

Good grief, I would rather risk whatever dental decay is going on in my mouth than take the time to floss, because (this is said in a whiny, self-pitying sort of way), "I'm tired." I feel no shame using this example, because I know most of you avoid flossing too.

Here's what it comes down to: we don't want to be inconvenienced.

Whether it's the oil level in my truck or an old wound that's lingering under the surface in my heart, I don't want the information that I already sense could be bad, don't want the disruption it could bring. I'd rather avoid it altogether. Until my car shuts down a hundred miles from home or I find myself deep into an addiction I know is rooted in unhealed pain.

Lord Jesus, I want to shift my posture in this. I want to stop avoiding disruption. I want to be willing to have a look under the hood whenever and wherever you are prompting me. I want to cultivate a willingness to go wherever it is I need to go to face my life. Especially when it comes to the internal issues. I love my old Land Cruiser, but it's a pretty small thing when compared to my heart and my walk with you. I give my yes to you now.

Dear friends, this may be one of the essential differences between those who experience God and the life he offers, and those who don't.

Be willing to have a look.

Now Is the Time

God gives us dozens of these encounters every day, these opportunities to be honest about what motivates us. What we do with them is up to us.

This is how he honors us. When God created each of us, he gave us a will, and that beautiful and mysterious inner life we call the soul. Just as you would want to give your growing son or daughter room to make his or her own decisions, God steps back a bit to let us make ours. These simple moments of decision are filled with significance. When I choose to avoid whatever it is God has brought up, something in me weakens. Something feels compromised. It is at least a refusal to mature. But it also feels like a refusal to step toward God. Thankfully, the opposite is true. When I choose to face the uncertain, admit the neglect, or enter into my fears, something in me grows up a little bit. I feel strengthened. The scales tip toward a closer walk with God.

Whatever else we do with these moments, let us be honest about one thing—there is no getting to it later. We don't get to it later. It simply goes away. And I wonder—how often do we say to ourselves, *I'll get to it later*, knowing that it will never happen, and thus we appease our conscience in the moment *and* avoid the issue, let it slip away under the ruse of "later."

So, how do we walk with God in the day to day, in the moment?

We go with it. Now. As it is unfolding. That is the only way to have any real relationship with Jesus Christ. I had to seize the moment on the porch in the rain and go with what God was bringing to the surface. It would have been easy to ignore it. But I would have missed what God was doing. I had to face the warfare when it struck, deal with the enemy, pray then and there. Otherwise, I would have lived under that malaise for who knows how long. I saw a window of opportunity with Anne at dinner, a chance to offer her the life and joy of Christ. Part of me wanted to ignore that opportunity, offer some banal word of encouragement, and get back to my pasta. But we would have missed a beautiful breakthrough.

Now is the time, dear friends.

Rest

There's a cool breeze blowing this afternoon, and the skies are cloudy. The breeze is coming from the west, and it soothes across my face as I sit here on the picnic table looking west to the Flat Tops. It smells different up at the ranch now—the lupine is gone and the sage isn't as pungent as it is in July when it's hot. The seasons are about to change. I can sense it in the earth. Things are quieter in a "summer's finished" sort of way.

I love this in-between time. My camp director days of summer are over. No one is asking me anything. The opening of archery season is not until next weekend. There is nothing to be done. The things I've done today I've done only because I wanted to. Chopped some wood. Fed the horses.

It's so quiet. And I absolutely love it. No e-mail. No phone to answer. My cell phone doesn't get reception here. Everyone I know is at least four hours away. Maybe I'll make a peanut butter and jelly sandwich for dinner because I don't want to make dinner.

And the best part of the peace and quiet is God. Just to sit here and be with God. No agenda. Nothing to be fought for or prayed over. Just God. It's like nothing else. Nothing even comes close. This is what the moment offers now. This is what God is up to today. And thankfully, I am going with it now, by resting with him.

Maybe tomorrow I'll fish. If that's what he has in store.

What God Is Giving

Earlier this summer my son Luke and I discovered a great little stream. It runs hard and fast down out of the Flat Tops, broken by old beaver dams and an occasional deep pool. Now and then it flattens out into lovely runs. We had a wonderful time catching wild rainbows and brook trout, much larger than I expected to see in that little stream. But we only had time to fish about a mile of it. I've been wanting to get back ever since and explore more of what this little treasure has to offer. I noticed on a map that the creek meanders far from the road before it spills into the Bear River, and there's nothing that catches a fisherman's imagination like the possibility of untouched waters. I might be the first guy to fish that section in years.

But I've done some releasing this summer. Things are beginning to ease up down inside. So I pray, *Jesus, is this a good day for fishing, or should I just lay low, hang out here?* I pause and listen. I'm really okay with either answer. *What do you think, Lord?* I listen, open to anything else he might want to say. For I've also learned this: sometimes God wants to speak to me about something entirely different than the question I'm asking. If I don't get an answer on the subject I've raised, I may need to ask a different question. You'll find this very helpful in learning to walk with God. If he doesn't seem to be answering the question you're asking, stop, and ask him what he *does* want to speak to.

Today, I am willing to surrender. Even fishing, which for a recovering fishing addict is a pretty good sign that God is at work. I sit quietly and repeat the question. *Jesus, shall we fish? What do you have for today?*

I hear, *Fish.*

My plan was to hike up the Bear to the confluence and begin my explorations from there. But the canyon of the Bear caught me by surprise. It's beautiful down in there. The river flows through a forest of evergreens, some of them leaning way out over the water so that the sunlight comes through here and there, splashing the river with light and shade. The river separates now and then into braids and then rejoins itself.

Now, it wasn't my plan to fish the Bear—I was after the untouched waters of the creek. But when I reached the bottom of the canyon and started upriver, I was immediately met with a handsome run of clear green water just begging for a dry fly. It was too inviting. I caught a lovely thirteen-inch rainbow on my first cast and made a change of plans. I would fish the Bear as I hiked—not too seriously, because the creek was my destination—but enough to sample the most alluring runs.

The Bear proved to be the treat of the day. By the time I reached the creek, I'd caught a half-dozen fish without much effort. And now that I'd reached my goal, it became obvious that the creek was unfishable. It plunges off a geologic shelf for a mile or so, cascading down with far too much speed to make for good fishing. I was disappointed. The creek was the point; the river had only been tossed in as a bonus. Or so I thought.

Then I remembered something that God has been teaching me this summer—it's not what he isn't giving but what he *is* giving. We can get so locked onto what we don't have, what we think we want or need, that we miss the gifts God is giving. Really, though the river had proved to be everything I hoped the creek would be—solitude, beauty, wild fish on a dry fly—I sulked halfway back to the car because I didn't get my creek.

Back in June I was obsessed with finding elk antlers on our property. I know there are some magnificent bulls that migrate through in the spring—when the elk shed their antlers—and being on private property, I knew my chances were pretty good of finding a trophy antler lying in the dense timber or along a fence line.

I set out one afternoon to hunt sheds with the prayer, *Father, I know you love me. Would you help me find a shed?* As I wandered up the bluff behind the cabin, I tried to listen to God for any guidance he might give. And it did feel as though at several junctures of game trails I was prompted to go right more than left or push higher up through the timber.

I was optimistic. As I crested the ridge, I had to push through a stand of young firs, and there ahead of me was a huge red-tailed hawk sitting on the top of a small fir, its back to me, swaying in the wind. He didn't know I was there, so I got to watch him for fifteen minutes or so. Every once in a while a gust of wind would sweep up the bluff and the hawk would spread his wings to maintain balance. Or was it to show me his beautiful brown and white pinions? Then suddenly he was in the air and off across the valley. A lovely gift. I knew it was a gift. And I had to say to myself, *It's not what God is not giving, but what he is giving.* No shed. But a hawk. He knows I love hawks. I collect their feathers. Will stop whatever I'm doing to watch them. This was today's gift. God did lead me, just not to what I expected.

Later, in July, my family and I were canoeing the Snake River in Teton National Park. This trip was an intentional move toward joy. We absolutely love that place. It was evening, and I was guiding our family and some dear friends down a part of the river most folks don't get to see and rarely canoe at dusk. I knew we would be alone, at the prime time for wildlife to come down for a drink. Hopes were high of seeing bull moose, elk, and who knows what else. We had seen bear in here before too. The evening could not have been more beautiful. As we glided along the banks, peering into the wild growth on either side, time slipped away. It could have been the 1800s. It could have been the 1600s.

We were utterly alone on the silent river, at twilight, and I knew we were in for a treat.

We passed the den of some river otters we'd seen last year. Nobody home. We passed the island that moose are always hanging out on. Nope. Just a beaver or two. Frustrated, I made the group paddle an extra mile through a back channel where I *knew* the moose had to be. But no. The sun passed behind Mount Moran, and everyone was enjoying a spectacular sunset in the clouds above. But I missed it entirely, because I was so disappointed we didn't see wildlife. I was totally focused on what God was *not* giving, and missed what he *was* giving. Only later, looking at the photos Blaine took, did I see all that I missed. The sunset was truly stunning. Peaches and violets and reds above the black silhouette of the mountains, all reflected in the river. I missed it. I nearly missed the Bear River today.

Father, forgive me. Forgive my demanding posture that life has to come to me on my terms. Oh Lord, how many gifts have I missed? Forgive me. The posture is ugly and narrow. I pray for a more gracious posture, to be open and grateful for what you are giving at any time. I pray to be your son.

On Elk and Elijah

The only thing worse than being cold is being cold and wet.

Opening day of archery season for elk comes at the end of August here in Colorado. It's a day we look forward to all year. Come June and July we start preparing, getting all our gear together, packing and repacking, talking through our plans for opening morning. Dozens of times over. (Often the greatest joy of an adventure is in the anticipation.) We came up to the ranch a few days ahead of opening weekend to scout for elk, and because like schoolboys about to be released for the holidays we weren't good for much of anything else, so we figured we may as well head out. Our hopes were soaring this year—we found the elk in good numbers, we knew where they were, and we knew how to get there. This was going to be great.

I awoke on opening morning to the sound of rain on the roof of the cabin. Lots of rain. It started about 4:00 a.m. and hadn't let up. To see the four of us sitting around as dawn began to break, you'd have thought it was raining in the house. We looked as woebegone as dogs locked in the kennel while the family drives away. I was thinking, *Thief. The thief of joy.* We were supposed to be out on the mountain by now, in position on opening morning, the best opportunity of the season. And so we started praying for the weather to clear.

Pause. One of my favorite Old Testament stories is the one about Elijah praying for rain. (Yes, I realize we had rain at the moment. Plenty of rain. What we needed was no rain. But hang with me. It works.)

Elijah climbed to the top of Carmel, bent down to the ground and put his face between his knees.

"Go and look toward the sea," he told his servant. And he went up and looked.

"There is nothing there," he said.

Seven times Elijah said, "Go back."

The seventh time the servant reported, "A cloud as small as a man's hand is rising from the sea."

So Elijah said, "Go and tell Ahab, 'Hitch up your chariot

and go down before the rain stops you.'" Meanwhile, the sky grew black with clouds, the wind rose, a heavy rain came on. (1 Kings 18:42–45)

I love it that Elijah kept sending his servant to have a look. Is it working? I love it that it took this mighty man seven rounds of prayer to get it going. This story is so true to life. And now for the really wild thought: James says we can do it too. Toward the end of his epistle, James is trying to encourage us to pray like we mean it. After the famous passage, "The prayer of a righteous man is powerful and effective," James points to this story as the example: "Elijah was a man just like us. He prayed earnestly that it would not rain, and it did not rain on the land for three and a half years. Again he prayed, and the heavens gave rain, and the earth produced its crops" (5:16–18).

Now – why did James make a point of saying that Elijah "was a man just like us"?

Because of that thing in each of us that says, *I could never do that.* Because of that theology that says, "Those stories are exceptions." That sort of thinking cripples faith. It cuts your prayer life off at the knees. Why are we given stories about the power of godly people praying if our prayers really don't accomplish anything? James said that Elijah was just like you and me. This was no exception. Meaning, you can pray and do this too. You can pray and see things happen.

Now remember—how many times did Elijah have to take a whack at it? Did he see results on the first round? The second? The third?

Too many times our prayers are wimpy little prayers like, "Jesus, be with us." He is with you. Always. Or we pray, "Lord, give us good weather today." And that's it. One round and we quit. And then we are discouraged when our prayers don't seem to do anything, and we come to the conclusion that prayer really doesn't work. It would be more accurate to say prayers like *that* don't work. Start praying like Elijah, and maybe you'll see some results.

(More at walkingwithgod.net)

So I am up, and pacing around the very small room we're in, and I am praying for the weather to clear. I keep looking out the window, like Elijah's servant, not for a cloud but for a break in the sky. There isn't any, so we keep praying. Now, I don't know where the weather is coming from. I don't know that God doesn't have something in it for us. I don't know if my prayers will help the day. All I know is that something that means a lot to us is being stolen.

Joy being stolen—that should always set off our alarm. I also knew that God loves it when we step out in faith. I knew he could sort out my prayers and use them any way he wanted. I also knew I wasn't just going to sit there and do nothing. So I prayed—hard.

I'd love to say that Blaine looked to the sea and saw a break in the clouds the size of a man's hand, but it didn't happen that way. I do know, however, that in about twenty minutes the rain began to ease up just a bit, and we decided to head out. In spite of the weather, we grabbed our gear, broke up into pairs, and began to implement the plans we'd made.

But this is not a story about our faith. Actually, it's about our remarkable capacity for unbelief.

We are now huddled under the boughs of a spruce tree, high

on the mountain, trying to get out of the rain. We have lost all hope of elk. There are no elk. Not on this mountain. There never have been. Why are we carrying bows? All there is is cold. And wet. The ground is cold and wet. The tall grasses are cold and wet. We are cold and wet. All the world is cold and wet. Yes, we had seen elk. We jumped *three* different herds on our way to this very point. An hour ago there were elk before us and behind us. But now, there are no elk. Never have been. Never will be. All that exists is cold and wet.

And then, the sun comes out. I kid you not.

We rejoice. We come out from under the boughs of the tree, and decide to hike back down into the gulch below us, believing that if there are any elk in the region, that's where they are going to come out. The sun is now beating down on us, and we heat up during our hike and start peeling off layers. By the time we reach the bottom of the mountain, we are hot. All the misery of the morning is gone. The world is filled with sunlight. We were cold? What is cold? I can't remember. There is no rain. Never has been. Now there is only hot. And I'm thirsty.

I am also stunned at my total loss of object permanence—the understanding that just because you can't see a thing right now doesn't mean it no longer exists. You can't see the stars during the day. They vanish from sight. But they haven't gone anywhere. They are still there. The elk are still somewhere on this mountain. Why do I so easily lose heart? I know I do this with God. When his sun is shining on me, so to speak, I am there. I *believe*. But when a cloud comes over—fear, doubt, or some awful event—the sun is gone. My faith is gone.

Lord Jesus, forgive me. How fickle I must seem to you. How utterly swayed by what seems real in the moment. Forgive me. Heal this in me.

I take some comfort in the rest of Elijah's story. Before praying up a rainstorm, he called down fire from heaven and had 450 prophets of Baal put to the sword. It hadn't rained for three years, yet that afternoon he called in a monsoon. Then he ran for his life from his enemies. God found him on a mountain in a mood of almost total unbelief.

"What are you doing here, Elijah?"

He replied, 'I have been very zealous for the LORD God Almighty. The Israelites have rejected your covenant, broken down your altars, and put your prophets to death with the sword. I am the only one left, and now they are trying to kill me too.'" (1 Kings 19:9–10)

It was all gone. There was no fire from heaven. There was no rain. It was all gone.

Maybe we're not so different after all.

"My Love"

Often as I move through my day and through my week, I'll turn my heart and my thoughts toward God simply to ask him, *What are you saying, Lord?* It's a way of checking in, giving God the opportunity to speak into whatever is going on, or to say whatever it is he might need to say to me. Driving down the road, sitting in a meeting, or taking out the trash, I ask, *What are you saying, Lord?* I'm just checking in. Paul says, "Since we live by the Spirit, let us keep in step with the Spirit" (Galatians 5:25). I suppose this is my attempt to keep in step.

For the past two months at least, what God has been saying

in return is *My love*. Every time I've stopped to listen, I've heard, *My love*. Over and over again, *My love*. And I've wondered why. When there are so many things going on in the world and in my life, so many things I know I need to hear from him, still he says to me, *My love*.

I haven't really known what to do with this. At first it was a comfort. What a wonderful thing to hear. My heart would sort of soften and say, Yes, your love. Thank you for your love. But after several weeks of this—we're talking months now—it began to bug me. That's it? The same thing? Your love? What, am I an idiot or something? Am I even hearing right? Why are you saying the same thing over and over?

After I got through that phase, God's words began to be a great source of comfort and orientation. They have brought me back again and again to his love. Right. This is all about your love. If I get nothing more, no further explanation, I'm okay with that. I can just sit with *My love*. But to be honest, I still don't think I'm getting it. God is repeating this for a reason. I do get that. But I'm not really sure why. It seems he's after something.

fall

winter
spring
summer

*a season of crisis and struggle, but
then breakthrough and discovery*

The Accident

When I came to, I was lying facedown in blood.

I could hear someone speaking. After a moment I recognized the voice. Stasi was asking, "Are you all right?"

Am I all right? "My nose is broken," I said. "And I think my right wrist is too. I can't tell about the left." I was doing the inventory your brain naturally races through when you have been hurt. *I can move my legs. And my arms. My head hurts, but I think it's okay. My nose is definitely busted. It feels huge. And there is something wrong with both wrists. I must have gotten thrown.*

It was Labor Day weekend. The boys were back in the woods building a tree fort, so Stasi and I decided to take a ride. We were headed up through a lovely though narrow aspen draw when my horse started acting skittish. I stopped and patted him on the neck. "Everything's okay, buddy." There's an old woodpile in this draw, and sometimes the horses don't like going by it. So, just as I'd done several times in the past month, I sat there to give S'mores time to figure things out, let him see for himself there wasn't anything waiting to get him in there. Every other time we'd come to this place, he had calmed down in a few moments and we had walked on through.

But not today.

S'mores spooked, wheeled on his hindquarters, and took off like a bottle rocket. He's a big horse (more than sixteen hands) with long legs, and let me tell you, we were moving fast. Stasi's horse followed suit. I started to come out of the saddle on the initial turn, regained my stirrup, and thought, *Hey, maybe I'm going to make it.* I started trying to slow him down, but the next thing I knew, I was waking up facedown in a pool of blood. Stasi was thrown too. Bruised, but not badly. I was a mess. But so much adrenaline was pumping through my injured body, I didn't realize how much pain I was in.

We had no idea where the nearest emergency room was, and I wasn't sure I needed to go. Stasi started calling neighbors. *Should I even go?* I ask. I don't want to go. I hate hospitals. I hate being in need. Maybe it's not too bad.

Go, God said. And it was a good thing I did. The broken nose wasn't too big of a concern. Neither was the fracture in my left wrist. But my right wrist was dislocated, and we were about to find out that it was a pretty serious injury, requiring surgery. I would be in a cast for nine weeks. Six of those weeks my left wrist was going to be in a cast too. This was going to change a lot.

Now, I know what you're thinking: *Did he ask God about the ride? Is that the lesson of this story?*

I don't remember if we did, actually. I've struggled a lot, trying to sort through what happened that morning. I know that during my morning prayers that day I had prayed against the thief of joy. I hadn't ever done that before. That's suspicious. I know that there was a lot of warfare around the ranch that weekend. I think we might have asked God about the ride, but I know we didn't ask *where* we should ride.

Pause. That's a really important part of listening to God, by the way. Ask the *next* question. So often we get an answer to the first part of a question but fail to ask the second half. We hear, *Yes, take the job,* or *Yes, sell the house.* But then we need to ask, *When? Today, next week, next year?* Don't just get a first impression and then blast ahead. It might have been good for us to ask, *Where should we ride?*

But it's a little late for that now. And you can really chase your tail on this sort of thing and get nothing but all tied up in knots. When it comes to crises or events that really upset us, this I have learned: you can have God or you can have understanding. Sometimes you can have both. But if you *insist* on understanding, it often doesn't come. And that can create distance between you and God, because you're upset and demanding an explanation in order to move on, but the explanation isn't coming, and so you withdraw a bit from God and lose the grace that God *is* giving. He doesn't explain everything. But he always offers us himself.

Besides, it happened. Now I'm all busted up. If there are lessons to learn from what happened, I trust God to reveal those in time. What I am watching for now is what comes next. What will I do with this? What will God do with this? How am I to walk with God *now*?

Right now, what I'm aware of is how shaken I am by what happened. I realize that my life is going to be radically changed for some time. I'm heartbroken as I start realizing the losses that come with this. I've lost archery season, all that time with Blaine and the guys. I can't tie my shoes, let alone pull a bow. Sam and I have been rebuilding his first car together, and now that's lost for who knows how long. I won't be able to help. I *really* want God to heal me. And I am very aware of how much I don't want to be in a place of need.

My whole approach to life has been built on be tough, need nothing, push through. I hated wearing that little hospital gown, the one that doesn't really tie in back. I insisted that Stasi put my boots on for me when it was time to leave. As we drove home from the emergency room in Steamboat Springs, my cell phone began to ring. Stasi had called a friend on the way to the hospital to ask for prayer. Word got out, and friends began checking in. I was completely blown away by the amount of love and concern. And I noticed something.

I have a *really* hard time being loved.

It's hard to accept a fundamental reorientation of one's approach to life. The old ways are so deeply woven into our personalities, so grounded in our core assumptions, so rooted in our wounds and in what has worked for us over the years. And there is nothing like a crisis to expose all of it. So long as our old ways are working, we really aren't open to looking at them. Let alone giving them up. But then something like this happens. Now I'm backed into a corner. This disruption is going to be far more than physical. Whatever else may come out of this, I want to be transformed. Love is pretty central to life, after all. I don't think it's a good idea to miss out on love.

I can't drive. I can't open a door. Opening a bottle of juice is impossible. So is cutting a steak. Oh man, I am going to need help with *everything*. I can't even button a button. Whatever else might be going on, this accident is thwarting my entire approach to life. I see it now. My approach to life is fundamentally based upon attack. That's how I live. I attack life. I get up in the morning and attack the day. Whatever needs to get done, whatever worries I may have, whatever fears lie underneath, I attack.

But that is not the life I want to live. And so I pray, *I come back to your love. You said, My love. I want a life that is based on your love. Rooted and grounded in your love.*

It's hard to say clearly enough or with enough force just how important this revelation is. Words like *paradigm shift* or *epiphany* just don't quite touch it. As we drove back down the highway from the hospital, me stretched out in the back of the Suburban, I prayed, *God, I give you permission to rebuild my personality based upon your love.*

God?

I am really struggling with this.

I know God loves me. Why wouldn't he just do this for me?

As soon as I got home from the accident, friends came over to pray. We prayed for healing. Earnestly. Fervently. For the next several days, we pray for healing. You see, the emergency room called in a hand specialist, and he was able to reset the dislocation. But now I need to go in for surgery. And I really don't want to. I want God to heal me. I have faith that he could. I believe he would want to.

But it didn't happen. I go in for surgery tomorrow.

Is the church impotent? *So* many people praying can't get this done? Why is that?

Why can't we heal, Jesus?

I am really disappointed. I have lost archery season. Lost the joy of hunting for this year. I can't get my hands on Sam's car. I'm just really, really disappointed. I wanted God to come through, not just for my heart, but for the hearts of my sons and my wife and so many other people. My healing would have been such an encouragement for their faith.

What am I to do with this, Jesus? I know there are many people hurting much more than I am. But still, I asked you for healing. Jesus, I need your help with this. Come to my heart in this.

And all the while, in the midst of struggle, I know I have to be careful. This is the vulnerable moment. This is when agreements seem so reasonable, so inescapable.

We have to be careful with our hearts in this very moment, when we are struggling deeply. I know I cannot give my heart over to anything. "Above all else, guard your heart, for it is the wellspring of life" (Proverbs 4:23). The spirit of the passage is this: you've got to be really careful what you give your heart over to. And of what you let in your heart. In the midst of this struggle, I know I cannot make agreements with anything. Not discouragement. Not unbelief. Not striving. Not resignation.

It would be so easy to make a subtle agreement down inside, like *Why bother? Prayer doesn't really do anything.* I don't want to go there. I don't know what all God is doing or why it seems at times that our prayers are impotent, but I know this—the only safe place for my heart is in God. Understanding or not, that is where I have to land. I've been through enough hard things to know that eventually there is light on the other side. In the meantime, I know we can shepherd our hearts. We have to.

No agreements.

Until God Becomes Our All

"How do we best understand life?"

I was meeting with a young woman the other day, talking through some hard times in her life. I don't know yet how to make sense of my accident or the fact that both my arms are now in casts. But life goes on, and I had to go to work. So I was meeting with this young woman who was dealing with some distress of her own, when she asked me what I thought was the truest way of looking at life. "My husband thinks life is just hard. I'm feeling that it's sort of random. We're not really good for each other right now. What do you think?" Oh, the beautiful timing of God. I am suddenly aware that Someone else is in the room. There is a sort of pregnant expectation in the air. What would I say? What *do* I believe?

"God wants us to be happy," I said. "But he knows that we cannot be truly happy until we are completely his and until he is our all. And the weaning process is hard." Even though I was playing the role of counselor in that moment, I was feeling that God had arranged the whole encounter for me.

"The sorrows of our lives are in great part his weaning process. We give our hearts over to so many things other than God. We look to so many other things for life. I know I do. Especially the very gifts that he himself gives to us—they become more important to us than he is. That's not the way it is supposed to be. As long as our happiness is tied to the things we can lose, we are vulnerable."

This truth is core to the human condition and to understanding what God is doing in our lives. We really believe that God's primary reason for being is to provide us with happiness, give us a good life. It doesn't occur to us that our thinking is backward. It doesn't even occur to us that God is meant to be our all, and that until he is our all, we are subhuman. The first and greatest command is to love God with our whole being. Yet, it is rare to find someone who is completely given over to God. And so normal to be surrounded by people who are trying to make life work. We think of the few who are abandoned to God as being sort of odd. The rest of the world—the ones trying to make life work—seem perfectly normal to us.

After the accident, I was really disappointed that life was suddenly beyond my grasp. Literally. The forecast for the next several months looked bleak. But do I ever feel this disappointed when God seems distant, when I seem to be losing my grasp of *him*? What is it with us? I am just stunned by this propensity I see in myself—and in everyone I know—this stubborn inclination to view the world in one and only one way: as the chance to live a happy little life.

Now don't get me wrong. There is so much about the world that is good and beautiful even though it is fallen. And there is so much good in the life that God gives us. As Paul said, God has richly provided us with everything for our enjoyment (1 Timothy 6:17). In Ecclesiastes, Solomon wrote that to enjoy our work and our food each day is a gift from God (2:24). We are created to enjoy life. But we end up worshiping the gift instead of the Giver. We seek for life and look to God as our assistant in the endeavor. We are far more upset when things go wrong than we ever are when we aren't close to God.

And so God must, from time to time, and sometimes very insistently, disrupt our lives *so that* we release our grasping of life here and now. Usually through pain. God is asking us to let go of the things we love and have given our hearts to, so that we can give our hearts even more fully to him. He thwarts us in our attempts to make life work so that our efforts fail, and we must face the fact that we don't really look to God for life. Our first reaction is usually to get angry with him, which only serves to make the point. Don't you hear people say, "Why did God let this happen?" far more than you hear them say, "Why aren't I more fully given over to God?"

We see God as a means to an end rather than the end itself. God as the assistant to our life versus God *as* our life. We don't see the process of our life as coming to the place where we are fully his and he is our all. And so we are surprised by the course of events.

It's not that God doesn't want us to be happy. He does. It's just that he knows that until we are holy, we cannot really be happy. Until God has become our all, and we are fully his, we will continue to make idols of the good things he gives us. We are like a child who throws a fit because he cannot have a toy or watch TV. In the moment, he could care less that his mother adores him. His world is out of sorts. He does not see that his heart is not in the right place. He needs his mother's love and comfort far more than he needs the thing he's made an idol of.

Whatever else might be the reason for our current suffering, we can know this: "The LORD your God is testing you to find out whether you love him with all your heart and with all your soul" (Deuteronomy 13:3). We are so committed to arranging for a happy little life that God has to thwart us to bring us back to himself. It's a kind of regular purging, I suppose. A sort of cleansing for the soul. I have to yield not only all my hopes for this fall, but my basic approach to life as well. Of all tests, I do not want to fail this one.

Now, I am *not* suggesting that God causes all the pain in our lives. I don't believe he pushed me off my horse to make a point. In fact, I believe he saved my life. But pain does come, and what will we do with it? What does it reveal? What might God be up to? How might he redeem our pain? Those are questions worth asking.

Don't waste your pain.

Making Room for God

After the accident I felt as though God wanted me to quit drinking.

Now, it's not like I drink a lot. I have a drink now and then. And I hate the feeling of being drunk, so I never drink to excess. But some of you are thinking, *One drop is more than the good Lord would be pleased with.* Why, then, did Jesus turn water into wine when the supply ran out at a wedding reception? Why did he go so far as to provide between 120 and 180 gallons of it? And really excellent wine at that. The act itself was an act of approval, of celebration. Let the party continue. So let's get this straight—the Bible does not condemn drinking. Drunkenness, yes. Drinking, no.

However, it had become to me something it ought not to be.

Sometime earlier this year, I noticed I was drinking too often, or more precisely, drinking for the wrong reasons. I'd come home exhausted and frazzled from the day, and I'd turn to a glass of wine or a beer as a sort of refuge and relief, a way to find some peace. Some people use food. Or television. For me it was alcohol. And that's not good. I began to see it as reaching for joy—

joy in a bottle, joy within my grasp. Yikes. This does not have a good future written on it.

And so God gave me a kind of grace to give it up. To make room in my life for him. It was really that simple. I noticed that when I came home frayed and weary, what I wouldn't do was simply take a few moments to be with God and ask him to comfort me, to be my refuge and peace. I decided to try that instead.

And so something I've enjoyed over the years is gone now. And I have no idea if or when it will return. What I notice is a kind of spaciousness now in my soul in the evening. Room for God.

A Sanctified Life

"Remain in me, and I will remain in you," Jesus said (John 15:4). A simple command, it seems. And yet, we overlook it.

If Jesus must tell us to remain in him, then he seems to be assuming that it is quite possible *not* to remain in him. The common life is, in fact, a life lived separate from him. And that is a dangerous place to live. We cannot enjoy the fellowship of God, or his protection, or all the benefits of his kingdom unless we remain in him—that is, live in him—in our day-to-day lives. Vine and branches, Shepherd and sheep. *Stay close. Stay with me,* Jesus is saying. An old saint said to me years ago that the devil doesn't so much care what particular thing he gets us to fall prey to. His primary aim is simply to get us to do something outside of Christ, for then we are vulnerable.

I want two things that are mutually opposed—I want to live a nice little life, and I want to play an important role in God's kingdom. And it's in those times that I am trying to live a nice little life that I make decisions and choices that cause me in small and subtle ways to live outside of Jesus. The Shepherd is headed one direction, and I am headed another. Not to some flagrant sin—that's too easy to recognize. Instead, I'm simply wandering off looking for the pasture I deem best. I don't even think to ask God about it.

I do wonder how much this played into my accident.

We pray over our horses every time we ride, bringing them under the authority of Jesus Christ and under the kingdom of God. We bind away fear and rebellion and bring the peace of God upon them. And we did pray that morning. But sometimes when I'm praying, I can tell it's not really working. I have a sense that it hasn't broken through yet or hasn't been fully effective. After all, even Elijah didn't get it done in one whack. All this means is that we need to pray some more. Do it again. Seven times if necessary. But sometimes I don't want to pray anymore. I just want to get on with things. I felt like that the morning of the accident. It was a sunny day, and I was tired of praying. I just wanted to go for a ride like a normal person.

A very dangerous way of thinking.

As Christians we don't get to live a "normal" life, and accepting that fact in all the details of our lives is what allows us to remain in Jesus. I remember a friend admitting something like this about his family vacation, "I don't want to ask God if we're supposed to go to Hawaii this year. I just want to go." And so you can see how the collision of our desire to live a nice little life and our need to remain in Jesus can bring about a sanctification of our will, where all things truly are subjected to Christ.

But there's something we need to be honest about: part of us doesn't really *want* to hear what God has to say.

Really. Even after years of God's rescues and surprises and blessing upon blessing, there's a part of me that gets irritated when someone says, "Let's ask God." The act itself is a disruption. Sometimes it feels like grinding the gears. Stop? Now? Ask God? I'm bugged. That's part of it. And the other part is, if we do hear something, we'll have to obey.

I was reading the story of Joshua, and it stopped me in my tracks. My goodness, the Israelites received specific instructions from God all the way through the battle of Jericho—when to cross the river, how to cross the river, when to take Jericho, how to take Jericho. And it worked! *It worked.* You'd think they would have been convinced. This is how to follow God. But the next day comes and here they are, ready to take city number two, and you know what—they don't ask! It's not that they don't ask the second question, they don't even ask the first. They just charge ahead. And they pay for it. Dearly.

I know something of this. I don't ask because I don't want to know. If I know what God thinks, then I'm faced with the decision of whether to follow his counsel or not. What was initially just a quandary or a moment of confusion becomes an issue of obedience. I don't want that sort of clarity. Furthermore, I don't want God messing with my approach to life.

And so we come back to holiness. To ask is an act of holiness, because we are seeking to follow our Shepherd. To live by faith in him. Then we are faced with the choice to obey what we hear, and our holiness is deepened.

This "nice little life" thing is really in the way.

More than anything else, this is what causes me to simply wander off on my own, looking for greener pastures. I'm thinking now about how Jesus said, "I don't do anything except what the

Father tells me to do" (John 14:31, my paraphrase). This is what we are after. It requires a desire to live in God and a willingness to subject our wills to his. This is where we are made holy. I am not describing the abandonment of our desires, that posture of the soul that says (with resignation), "Just tell me what you want me to do and I'll do it." That's the easy way out. What I am describing is a heart that is present and engaged with God, bringing our desires to him, yet submitting our wills to his, genuinely trusting that what he says is best.

That is how we come to learn to remain in him.

The Agreements We've Made About Love

I'm thinking about love this morning.

I've been noticing that most mornings I don't wake up super-happy, and I'm not sure why. I've also been noticing for some time now that when I first wake up, I find myself racing through the coming day in my mind, bracing myself for what's required of me, but even more so searching to see if there is anything to look forward to. It's not really voluntary. It's almost as if my heart has a life of its own, and it wakes up before I do and begins to assess the prospects before me. "I slept but my heart was awake" (Song of Songs 5:2).

By the way, I think this is how our addictions get their claws deeper into us. Our day-to-day grind isn't anything close to Eden, and our hurting and desperate hearts look for something to which we can attach all those yearnings. We'll settle for a dough-nut if that's all there is to look forward to. We have to be careful what we give our hearts over to.

Anyhow, this is what happened this morning. I didn't wake up with songs of happiness in my heart, and I found myself searching for something to look forward to. (This as I stumbled toward the bathroom. It all took place within a few moments.) I don't want to give my heart to just anything that looks like hope, so I turn my thoughts to God, knowing, at least intellectually, that the only safe place for my heart is in the love of God. *Love. It's about love, remember?* I say to my heart. *Come back to love, my heart. To the love of God.* My self-talk helps, in that I begin to realign my heart with God. This turning in the right direction is almost like turning a ship around. It takes time for the soul to realign itself with God, and things are creaking and groaning, but slowly I am tacking into the wind.

As I turned my thoughts and the desire of my heart toward the love of God, turned my soul his direction (he is always waiting there), I noticed what seemed to be a twinge of pain. It felt, for lack of a better description, old, historic, deep-seated.

Have I made an agreement that I will never be loved? I wonder. The thought came partly through years of counseling others, partly through intuition, and maybe partly because someplace deep down in my heart that sentence keeps being repeated, and I can vaguely perceive it coming up from the depths. As I ask myself, *Have I made an agreement? Did I ever come to the conclusion I will never be loved?* something in my heart resonates, clicks. The thought seems to fit. So I know that this is something I need to chase after. Some healing is yet needed.

I know I'm not alone in having a hard time believing in the love of God for me (we think he loves everyone else), or receiving the love of God, or letting it catch my heart up into life and joy, or, maybe especially, staying there for any reasonable period of time. An hour or two would be amazing. A day would be a triumph. And I'm thinking that maybe part of the reason we have a hard time believing in God's love for us hides back in our story somewhere. I remember something Gerald May wrote years ago: we need to let ourselves tell *our* stories of love—how love came to us over the course of our lives, or how it did not come, or how it left. We need to tell the story so that we understand. And I remember thinking at the time, *No thank you. I'd rather not go there. Thanks just the same.*

And I ignored the issue for years.

Now I'm trying to bring my heart back to the love of God, let it heal me, and stay there. It feels sometimes like searching through a dark forest for a wounded deer and trying to coax it in so I can touch it.

Our story of love is a very tangled story about the most precious thing in our lives (our longing for love). It's a hard story to tell for two reasons. For one thing, we're too close to it to often have any clarity at all. Can't see the forest for the trees. More deeply, it's a heartbreaking story, and we're not sure we want to revisit the painful details. That's why we're ambivalent about love. Oh, we yearn for it. We want to be loved. But we hide from it too, building defenses against it, fortressing ourselves from being hurt again. We settle for a doughnut.

Then we wonder why it's hard for us to connect with the love of God, let it in so deep that it heals us, and remain in his love.

I need to come back to agreements. As I explained before, agreements are really subtle and nasty things. They pin our hearts down, or shut them down by handing over to the enemy a sort of key to a certain room in our hearts, and in *that* place he shuts the door and locks it. This is what's behind the impasses you find in otherwise healthy people's lives. Your friend Jane is a wonderful woman, loves God, leads mission trips. But she collapses internally whenever someone criticizes her. Goes into a depression and binges. Your brother Dan is a kind and loving man, one of the more mature men you know. But he hasn't returned your calls for three weeks because over dinner one night you asked him why he hasn't been dating anyone.

You've probably just run up against a wounded place in the heart held in bondage by an agreement, quite often having to do with love.

Think back over your story of love. In those moments when you were wounded you were really vulnerable for agreements to come in. They come swiftly, imperceptibly, often as a response to some message delivered with the wound. Your boyfriend breaks up with you. It hurts too much, so you shove the pain down and try to get away from it. But your heart is coming to conclusions. *It's all because of me. I'll never really be loved again.* And the thing is, you may not even be aware that you made the agreement. Our enemy is cunning, and after he secures the agreement, he drops the issue for a while, goes underground, lays low for awhile so that nobody discovers his work there. By "lays low for a while," I mean it could be thirty years or more. All you know is, you can't feel the love of God.

Standing in the bathroom with the shower running and empty, I wonder . . . *where and when did I make the agreement that I will never be loved?* I wonder . . . *how common is that agreement to the human heart?* I don't really know what else to do and I've got to get on with my day, so I prayed,

Jesus, okay. Okay. Come in here. I really want and need your love, much more deeply than I've allowed myself to let it in. I want to stay there, keep my heart in your love. Come and show me what sort

of agreements I've made about love. Show me where they are, when they came in. Help me to let them go. Renounce them. Accept your love instead. Oh, heal my fearful heart. I am willing to look at my story of love. Walk with me there.

Later, in my office, I sat for a while in silence. I didn't have any clarity, but I could sense rumblings within. The last thing I wanted to do was force this. That never brings the wounded deer close enough. So I sat and futzed with some other writing. Maybe that was enough on this for today. I did some spell checking. Looked out the window. My thoughts drifted off to bow hunting. A meeting I had later in the day. A phone call I forgot to make. But I knew I didn't want to go near the subject of making agreements about love, so I was careful not to justify my dissociation and just walk away. Finally, I came back to this issue with a question for myself: *What do I believe about love?*

That it never stays.

Whoa. Geez. *How long has that been there?* I wonder. Okay, I see it now. I do not trust love. I don't. That characterizes a lot of my life. *Jesus, come into this.* I sighed deeply and sat in silence again for a while, almost like mourning the delivery of some very somber news.

I knew it was true though—the revelation, that is. Didn't take a brain surgeon to figure out why I believed love never stays. Dad left. Alcohol took him away. Mom left. She had to go back to work to support us. Brent left. I realized, at least intellectually, that his death was not really him choosing to walk away from me. But still, he was gone. I could name a number of others, all who left. My life felt like a series of people leaving.

Jesus, what do I do with this?

Give it to me.

Okay. I give this to you Jesus. I let it go. Your love stays. I can

trust your love. I renounce the agreement I made that love never stays.
I invite you into the pain that brought it, all the losses. Come and
heal my heart in this place. Free my heart to trust in love, in your love.

Now I do have to go. But I want to treat this place gently,
think about it during the day, and return to it when I can.

The Next Day

That love thing really threw me yesterday. I mean, I wasn't looking to go there. It's such a vulnerable place. My story of love?
Good grief . . . it's too much. I just don't want to deal with it, sort
through all that. I'd rather keep my distance.

Maybe that's why God has to sneak up on us.

I am so aware—and I see it in all my friends—of this way of
living that says, *Don't disrupt me, don't take me into stuff I don't
want to deal with. Let me get on with my life.* Remember the Land
Cruiser? I don't even want to check the oil, let alone deal with my
story of love. *Just let me get on with my life.* And God, in all his
loving-kindness, says no. (And something in each of us says, *Dang.*
Or something more colorful. We know it's true. The hound of
heaven isn't so easily put off our scent.) God says to us, *We have
to go there. You are not well. Not whole and holy yet, not through
and through. I want you to have life, but you won't really have it
until you are whole and holy.*

We walk through the world too vulnerably when we refuse to
deal with the deep things of our hearts. Especially our story of love.

Here's what happened through the rest of the day yesterday.
A young man I know has been having a really hard time lately. It
has to do with his marriage. His wife is not a tender woman. There

is little love between them. He is really losing hope. The enemy has noticed his heartache (demons smell our struggles like sharks smell blood in the water) and moved in to make things worse. This is Satan's modus operandi—to seize upon our trials, weaknesses, or unhealed places and magnify them and try to set up shop there. Anyhow, this young man has his grief, but now a spirit of overwhelming sorrow is also jumping on board and pulling him under.

So he comes by yesterday and asks me if we could talk. I pray with him some, and while I'm praying I experience pain in my own heart. *Oh, so this is what the enemy is doing—he's piercing his heart with sorrow.* I can't begin to number how many times I've experienced this—someone else's spiritual oppression trying to jump on me. The stuff likes to transfer around. Like a computer virus. Just that morning, standing in the bathroom, I was made aware of one of the deep agreements I made about love, and so I'm a little tender and vulnerable as I go into my day. Now I'm in the arena with a spirit of overwhelming sorrow. Do you see how set up I am to become another victim of this heartache?

If you're not heads-up about this stuff, you get mugged.

It would have been easy for the story to have gone on like this: I see in his life that love doesn't work, doesn't stay; and I easily could have returned to the agreement I'd renounced only that morning. *See, it doesn't. Don't be a fool. You were right all along.* I would have lost the ground gained. And I would have to deal with his warfare as well, this spirit of overwhelming sorrow piercing my heart, assaulting me because I was trying to help him. If I wasn't aware of how warfare tries to transfer around, I could have experienced the heart piercing, thought it was related to my own sorrow, and let it in with the subtle agreement, *Yes, my heart does hurt. Life is sorrow and loss.*

Do you see what a dangerous world we live in? This is no Sunday school class. This is Vietnam, Kosovo, Baghdad. This is why God is so insistent that we deal with the unhealed and unholy places in our lives. He knows how vulnerable we are.

Thank God I had some sense of what was going on. I rejected the lie that this man's situation proved my former agreement about love. I brought the cross of Christ against his oppression and sent it from me to the throne of Christ. And now I am here this morning, out from under all that, and back to what God brought up without all the other trash trying to jump on. I am needing to return again to God's love, and what I need right now is just the truth—the objective, everlasting truth about his love for me. So I turn to the Scriptures.

> "I have loved you with an everlasting love;
>> I have drawn you with loving-kindness.
> I will build you up again
>> and you will be rebuilt. . . .
>> and go out to dance with the joyful." (Jeremiah 31:3–4)

Everlasting love—that cuts right through the lie that love never stays. His love does. It is everlasting. Immovable. True.

Oh yes, Lord. I long for your love. I would love to be joyful again.
I read a few more passages:

How great is the love the Father has lavished on us, that we should be called children of God! (1 John 3:1)

And hope does not disappoint us, because God has poured out his love into our hearts by the Holy Spirit, whom he has given us. (Romans 5:5)

I'm just using the references in my study Bible to go from one passage on the love of God to another, like a famished man let into a buffet.

"As the Father has loved me, so have I loved you. Now remain in my love." (John 15:9)

"No, the Father himself loves you because you have loved me and have believed that I came from God." (John 16:27)

"I have made you known to them, and will continue to make you known in order that the love you have for me may be in them and that I myself may be in them." (John 17:26)

Oh yes, God. This is what I want. For your love to be in me. I long for your love to fill my heart. What do I do?

I ask this because I'm not exactly feeling the love of God right now. My heart feels a little sad, with a touch of pain. How often this is true—I've seen it time and time again in the lives of the people I've counseled. We don't believe the Scriptures because they don't seem to align with what we are *feeling* right now. It has frustrated the livin' daylights out of me to see people clinging to their agreements and unbelief because that is what they are feeling in the moment. We are so stubborn in our unbelief because we aren't at that moment *experiencing* whatever it is God says is true. Now the roles feel reversed. Now I'm the doubting Thomas, and now I realize that the frustration and exasperation I often feel as a counselor is how God feels all the time.

Let this be true, God says. *Believe it. Make your agreement with me in this.*

What a beautiful invitation. He knows that we make agreements with all sorts of lies, distortions, and accusations. Now he invites us to agree with him in what is *true*.

We cannot base our convictions on whether or not we are feeling or experiencing the truth of what God says. It is an arrogant posture, to let our immediate state of being be the judge of whether the Scripture is true for us. I know I have to start with the truth, embrace it, stake my all on it, and then later—sometimes right away, sometimes down the road—I will experience its truthfulness. As Jesus said to Thomas, "Blessed are those who have not seen and yet have believed" (John 20:29).

Okay, okay, okay, okay, okay. Yes. This is what is true. I will let it be so. I make my agreement with you in this.

(More at walkingwithgod.net)

What I Have Been Praying

Several weeks have gone by since that morning in the bathroom when God raised the whole issue of love. I've been asking him what I should pray, and he has been replying, *That my love would heal your heart.*

Oh, how deeply he knows me. Knows me better than I know myself. And how true and good to pray just this. My heart does need his love and healing. He's also been saying, *Give me your heart.* The two go hand in hand. At first I was bugged by his persistence, bugged by the fact that he kept answering, *That my love would fill your heart, heal your heart.* But that only shows how much I do need healing, and also why and where I need God's love and healing.

While all of this has been going on this morning, another force has been tugging at me. I think the best way to put words to it is the phrase "Make it happen." I have no idea how deeply this runs in me. But it feels almost core to my personality. I gave God permission, when we were driving back from the hospital on Labor Day weekend, to rebuild my personality based on his love. Right now I don't feel that it's based on his love at all. It feels built upon Make It Happen.

We are back up at the ranch at the end of archery season. No, I'm not hunting. My hands are still in casts. I still can't even tie my own shoes. But I wanted to come back with the guys so that I could act as Blaine's guide. I can still hike. I can call in an elk. But it snowed again last night, and as I prayed about the day, God said, *Don't do it.* I could slip out there, and a fall would not be good right now. That Make It Happen thing in me would have me out with the guys in the cold and snow, trying to get an elk for Blaine. It would be hard, and I would be striving, and it would be stupid.

Even though my hands are both in casts, making it hard to make things happen, it's not impossible. I could miss this opportunity for transformation and just push through. But my soul needs healing here, in this. Even this morning, while praying and reading Scripture, flies were buzzing on the window, and I felt I should take a magazine and kill them. Take care of that. Like I could hit a moving object. I couldn't even hit a slug right now. But that doesn't occur to me. *I ought to get those flies* is but one of a hundred versions of Make It Happen.

Lord Jesus, have mercy. This is so deep in me. I hardly know what to do, what to say. Have mercy. Heal me here, in this. Heal me in your love.

Even while writing that last thought and prayer, I was struck by the thought, *What time is it? Four o'clock. I ought to be scouting for the guys by five.* Seriously. Right in the middle of the prayer. And then shortly after, I look out the window to see what the weather is doing (low clouds, cold, looks like snow soon), and I think, *I ought to get a better way of predicting the weather up here. I ought to get a weather band radio.* This is nearly constant. This sort of thinking, planning, anticipating, maneuvering comes so naturally. Seeing it so starkly now, I'm left speechless. May Jesus have mercy.

This morning I asked God what to read. He said, *Psalm 17.*

> I call on you, O God, for you will answer me;
>> give ear to me and hear my prayer.
> Show the wonder of your great love,
>> you who save by your right hand
>> those who take refuge in you from their foes.
> Keep me as the apple of your eye;
>> hide me in the shadow of your wings
> from the wicked who assail me,
>> from my mortal enemies who surround me. (verses 6–9)

The phrase "Keep me as the apple of your eye" really caught me. I love that passage. There is something young in me that resonates with that. It is the life of the beloved son, the very opposite of Make It Happen.

Jesus, I sanctify all of my gifts and all of my abilities to make it happen to you now. I bring them to you, Jesus, to serve you and not my godless approach to life. I ask that your love would heal that part of me that feels I must make it happen, that all things—especially my happiness—are up to me. I invite your love to come to this place and heal. And, Jesus, I repent of that part of me that needs to make things happen. I transfer my trust from my ability to make things happen to your love and goodness.

Dreams

I had the weirdest dream last night.

Then again, isn't that how everybody starts a story about a dream? "I had the weirdest dream last night." As if being on a roller coaster with King Tut might not be weird. What dreams aren't weird? "Weird dream" is sort of redundant. Anyway, back to the story.

We are still up at the ranch, but I dreamed about a place I used to work. In my dream I was still working there. (Which, I think, moves the dream into the category of nightmare.) To make matters worse, they had placed me in some sort of prison. I had just been released, but I was in a heated argument with my former boss, who felt they had done nothing unusual or unreasonable. "You can't do this to me!" I said. I told them I quit, and I remember even in my dream how incredibly good it felt to my soul. I woke up feeling a wonderful relief. "I quit!"

Okay, so it's not *that* wild to dream you're in prison in your job. You don't need a dream to tell you that you hate your job, that you feel trapped there. It did strike me as weird, though, because I haven't worked there for many years. But what is really wild is what follows. At breakfast this morning, Blaine says, "I had a really weird dream last night." (There it is again.) "I was with some other people, and we were on a rescue mission. To set you free. From that place you used to work."

Now, what would you do with that information?

What we typically do with stuff like this is raise our eyebrows and say, "That's really wild. Huh." And then we just head off into the day, never to give it another thought.

The guys are about to head out the door to hunt, but a light snow fell during the night. And though I really want to go along, I sense the Father saying that I should stay back at the cabin. Yield. Discretion being the better part of valor, I stay. They left, and I opened my Bible to spend some time with God. I am reading in Psalm 16 when I ran across this: "I will praise the LORD, who counsels me; / even at night my heart instructs me" (v. 7).

Wait a second. "Even at night my heart instructs me"? That little internal bell goes off. God is calling. I remember the dream. Then I also remember that driving up here, to pass the hours Blaine and I had listened to a book on tape, and in that story God was speaking to a young man through his dreams. Hello. My dream and Blaine's dream were important. God is saying something. I don't know what, but too many "coincidences" are coming together here.

Now, in our walk with God, this is the critical moment. Too often we merely say, "Wow. What a coincidence." We look at it like a two-headed rooster perched on our windowsill and then go have a sandwich. We never do anything with it. And so we lose the gift God is trying to give. Or miss the warning he is sending up like a flare.

I know I need to pray. Now. Before God's message slips away for a second time. And maybe the last. "Seek the LORD while he may be found," the Scriptures urge (Isaiah 55:6). In other words, now is the time. If I wait for some other time to make sense of this, pray about it, it won't happen. The rush of life will sweep it away.

Now is the time.

What do I pray, Lord? What is this about?

Pause. This is a really, really helpful place to begin—to ask God what to pray. I don't know what's going on. I'm looking at the equivalent of a two-headed rooster on my windowsill. I don't know why God brought this up. So I ask him. Remember the disciples asking Jesus, "Teach us to pray"? Too many times we just jump in and start praying (making prayer speeches to God), and it doesn't have much effect. We just sort of swing our sword around in the air randomly. Do this for a while and you'll get the impression that prayer doesn't really work. Or that God isn't in it. Oh, it works, and he's in it. When we pray effectively. John says, "This is the confidence we have in approaching God: that if we ask anything according to his will, he hears us. And if we know that he hears us—whatever we ask—we know that we have what we asked of him" (1 John 5:14–15).

That's an awesome promise. If we pray according to God's will, he hears us all right. And he answers our prayers. Isn't that what you want? I sure do. I want to see my prayers work! I want to pray according to God's will. But I don't always know what that is, so, *I ask*. This has absolutely revolutionized the way I pray. And I am seeing a lot more results, just as the scripture promised.

Back to the kitchen in the cabin and the two-headed rooster. What I sense God telling me to do is to bring the full work of Christ between me and this company, sever all spiritual bonds between me and them. Remember, the dream was about bondage, imprisonment, needing a rescue to be set free from that place. To understand the dynamic here, you need to understand something about spiritual authority. When you place yourself under a church (by joining it), or under a company (by taking employment there), you come under their spiritual authority. This can be good, or it can be bad. It depends on what the leaders choose to let in, spiritually speaking.

People coming out of cults often struggle with spiritual oppression until they sever all spiritual bonds with that cult and its leaders. Sadly, if an otherwise good church has given place to a strong spirit of religious pride, you'll often find that most of its members struggle with religious pride. It goes around, infecting everybody like the flu. The same dynamic holds true in families. Have you ever wondered why adultery or divorce or financial ruin seem to run in certain families? Because somewhere along the line, the leader of that family let it in, through sins and agreements, and it passes down the line until someone takes a stand against it.

What do I pray, Lord?

I sense God showing me that to be truly free from that place, and to move fully into my new calling, I need to bring the work of Christ between me and the organization, its leaders, and my former boss. So here is how I pray:

I bring the full work of my Lord Jesus Christ—his cross and shed blood, his resurrection and his life, his authority, rule, and dominion—between me and this place, and between me and all people there. Its officers and leadership and my former boss. I sever all spiritual ties between us, and I cancel any claims the enemy is making to me now because of my time spent there. I come out from under their authority. I consecrate my calling and my gifting to God. I cleanse my calling and gifting with the blood of Jesus Christ, to be holy and pure and filled with the Spirit of God alone. I keep the work of Christ between us and forbid these ties to be reformed. In the name and the authority of the Lord Jesus Christ.

Now, I don't know all that this accomplished in the spiritual realm, but even as I prayed, I could sense something lifting off of me. I felt freer. Lighter. And to think it all started with the weird "coincidence" of two dreams.

(More at walkingwithgod.net)

Listening on Behalf of Others

Yesterday was exhausting. A young woman we know and love has been increasingly distressed over the past few months, and it was time we stepped in to offer some prayer. She's a beautiful young woman who loves God, who also very much wants to be married, but until recently no young man had taken the initiative to pursue her. I don't know why. Finally, a man came into the picture. But as with most relationships, things were rocky and messy, and she began to grow increasingly distressed—tears, sleepless nights, distraught more often than not. Her friends began to feel that her reactions were out of proportion to the situation.

And that is a very important sign.

When you see in others—or find in yourself—reactions and responses that seem way out of proportion, that's a clue that something else is going on. Other things are at play. We usually just write such reactions off to immaturity, when in fact God may be using them to surface deeper issues so that we can deal with them. Or the enemy may be up to something. Quite often, both are going on. But what usually happens is that we're embarrassed by our overreaction, and we do what we can to quickly get past it. We leave the room. Hide what we're feeling. Hang up the phone as soon as possible. And often those around us want that as well—for us to "get over it." This was the growing consensus of those close to the young woman whose story I am telling. We'll call her Sally.

Sally came to me a few days ago, tears in her eyes and dark circles from lack of sleep. "I don't know what to do," she said. Now, I've noticed over the years that I have two reactions when someone is in distress. I feel uncomfortable, and want to get beyond the awkwardness as quickly as possible. This is what fuels our attempts to offer a quick word of comfort or advice, hoping to shift the conversation or get out of the room as quickly as we can. It's godless. It's cowardice. It is nothing less than retreat—a retreat from battles we don't know we can handle or don't *want* to handle, a retreat to try and get back to a nice little life as fast as we can.

I hate that part of me.

Thank God there is another response that's been growing in me over time, growing as Jesus comes to have more and more of me. I want to engage. I want to intervene. I want to help. I asked Sally what she felt was going on, wanted to hear her perspective on her distress. Was she aware that it seemed way out of proportion? Was she aware that this had one part to do with the young man and five parts to do with deeper issues in her soul? When it comes to helping another human being, you can treat the symptoms or you can treat the cause. Most people dabble in symptom management, and that is why most people don't seem to be getting better.

To cut this part of the story short, Sally was aware that her distress seemed rooted in something other than how things were going with the young man in her life. She asked if a few of us could pray and listen on her behalf.

Listening to God on behalf of one another may be one of the greatest gifts we can offer each other in the body of Christ.

If you haven't yet, you'll soon find that it is far easier to hear the voice of God for someone else than it is to hear it for yourself. I'm not sure all the reasons for that. Certainly one of them is that we're not emotionally tangled up in hearing. Sally was distressed. She couldn't hear what God was saying for the same reason you can't get a good night's sleep if you approach it by saying to yourself, *I have to get a good night's sleep.* There's too much pressure. You're not going to sleep. What a gift it can be, then, to take the pressure off by listening on one another's behalf.

A bit more on the dynamics of helping someone. In addition to keeping an eye out for what is going on in the hurting person's heart, you have to have your radar up for what the enemy is doing as well. Sally's friends were mostly irritated with her, the result being that they were not offering much help. Heads up! The enemy will do this to prevent help from coming. He will try and get *you* to do to them what *he* is doing to them. Even though we offered to pray for Sally, I suddenly wanted to put it off. I felt tired and irritated. Do not be fooled by this. Do not let it take you out. The night before the day of intervention, I had a lousy night of sleep. That's a good sign—the enemy is freaking out, knows his gig is up—and now the warfare is transferring to you. Don't let that deter you either. Take it as a sign that something good is going to happen. Breakthrough is on the way.

Sensing that there was a great deal of spiritual warfare involved, I knew the spiritual interference might make it hard to hear from God once we gathered with her. So I took some time to pray in advance as I was making coffee that morning. *Jesus, what's up?*

What's assaulting Sally? I heard Jesus say, *Desolation.* The spirit assaulting Sally was Desolation. But of course. You shall know them by their fruit.

My hunch was that Desolation was taking advantage of Sally's emotional distress. We began our time of prayer by bringing the work of Christ against Desolation, sending the spirit to the feet of Jesus. This took a couple rounds of prayer. It often does. After all, you are dealing with rebellious spirits. Once the air was cleared, we were able to pray for the places of deep inner brokenness in Sally, places broken by rejection when she was young. This is that dynamic I referred to earlier, where in Ephesians Paul warns, "Do not let the sun go down while you are still angry, and do not give the devil a foothold" (4:26–27). Long ago, in her story of love, Sally felt desolate. An agreement was made. Desolation came to stay.

That is, until today. We asked Jesus to come and to minister to the young and wounded places in Sally. She broke her old agreement with Desolation. And with the lie that she would never be loved. Jesus was very present. It was beautiful.

What was so sweet about the time of prayer was that several of us could listen and pray on Sally's behalf. *We* could hear the voice of God when she could not. But as we prayed over each thing Christ revealed, Sally began to come back to her true self. And she began to hear the voice of God. Oh, how I wish this kind of intercession was more widely practiced in the body of Christ. One of the richest treasures of learning to hear God's voice is the great good we can do for others. In fact, I think you'll find that listening for others will develop your ability to hear for yourself.

I wish that were the end of the story. It rarely is.

I got a call from Sally the next morning. She was in tears. The boy she was dating broke up with her that very night. We felt like we were about to lose all the ground we had gained and then some. All her old agreements were right there, waiting to rush back in, and the enemy with them. Thank God we acted when we did. If we had not gotten rid of Desolation and brought substantial healing to the old places of rejection, this would have been devastating. God moved us to intervene in the nick of time.

But the enemy was ticked. Right there in the phone call, I was hit with *I give up. This kind of prayer doesn't work. Forget it. God doesn't come through for people; healing doesn't really happen. Just back away from people.* Subtle but clear. An agreement with the very warfare this poor woman had been making agreements with herself—Desolation. After I hung up I had to renounce this. "No," I said out loud. "That is not true. I reject that feeling [that subtle despair often comes as a feeling], and I reject that lie. God is at work."

Later that evening, Luke—who is normally the happiest person in our family—was moping around the house. We tried to coax him out of it to no avail. Stasi recognized the warfare, and they prayed. The spirit didn't leave. I got involved, making the connection with Sally. (Remember, warfare works like a virus. It tries to transfer around as much as it can, especially when you've been involved in trying to set someone free.) The three of us prayed together against Desolation specifically. In about thirty minutes, Luke was back to being himself.

We can learn a couple of things from this experience. First, don't just assume the attack you are under on any given day is yours. It might be someone else's battle, trying to transfer to you. Sometimes it happens after you have been a help to them, and sometimes it comes *beforehand*, trying to take you out so that you don't even offer any help. Let this be a category for you when you realize you are under some form of attack. Ask, "Where is this coming from? Whose warfare might this be?" Ask God about it. Second, if you are going to love others well and intervene as we are called to intervene, you are going to have to be careful you aren't making the same agreements they are. You *will* be tempted to.

And so we are back to holiness.

We will be pressed, when we are helping others, to succumb to whatever it is that besets them. "Brothers," Paul says, "if someone is caught in a sin, you who are spiritual should restore him gently. But watch yourself, or you also may be tempted" (Galatians 6:1). The enemy will try to find a weakness—an old wound, an agreement, some fear or sin—to get you to give way so that you cannot help the person in need. As we are being pressed, we have an immediate opportunity to break any agreements we've made, repent of any sins we've committed, so that we might be whole and holy, so that we might help those we love. I find I have to do this in the moment, in the midst of the conversation or the prayer. *Lord, I've done the same thing. Forgive me. Cleanse me. I renounce the agreements I've made here.*

This gives us a new reason to pursue holiness—we might not always be able to rouse ourselves to fight the battle on our own behalf, but we may find a deeper resolve when it comes to loving others. Don't give way, don't surrender. You are needed.

Back to Joy

Are you beginning to see now how essential joy is?

Because we live in a world at war. *Because* the enemy is relentless. *Because* we are "hard pressed on every side" (2 Corinthians 4:8). For these very reasons we need joy. Lots and lots of joy. Bucketfuls. Wagonloads. Joy can counter the effect of all this unrelenting other stuff. Without it we'll get drained from the battle, sucked dry. We won't have anything to draw upon. No inner reserves. We'll waste away. Throw in the towel. Or we'll fall into an addiction because we are absolutely starved for joy.

I was reading back over my own life here in these stories, and I was thinking, *Good grief, how depressing. It's just battle after battle.* But it's not really. Now that I'm trying to be more intentional about it, or open to it, joy is coming my way too. Even though I didn't get to hunt this fall, I was able to make it into the woods several times with the guys. On a cold October weekend, Morgan and I called in a bull elk for my son Sam. It was the first great, successful hunt for us in more than ten years, and it was a day filled with adventure and joy. Yes, we had to pack it off the mountain through a couple miles of fallen timber. But that was a joy too.

And there are a lot of just ordinary days. Still, my need for regular joy is beginning to come clear.

The world's version of battle and joy is striving and indulgence. Push hard, and then reward yourself with a little something. Work like a dog, then buy yourself a big-screen TV. It's a cheap counterfeit of battle and a cheap counterfeit of joy.

If you walk with God, you will find yourself called up to the real thing. Intense battle. Authentic joy. The battle will find you. But you have to be intentional about the joy.

The Spirit of the Age

So, I've come back up to the ranch this late November weekend to check on things. Sitting here in the cabin, life feels so completely different. Normal—in the sense of this is how we were meant to live. The coffee tastes better up here. It's the same exact stuff I make at home, in the same cheap coffeemaker, but it smells fantastic and it's full of flavor. Why is that? Stasi and I were out to dinner in an upscale restaurant two nights ago and probably paid thirty bucks a plate, but the ninety-nine-cent noodles I just made coming back from hiking was the best food I've had in a month.

I hate the pace of my life.

I don't live. I get things done.

My life is entirely task oriented. I wake and pray, because if I don't pray, I get taken out by warfare. It's not leisurely prayer; it's purposeful prayer. I head to the office and start replying to e-mails. Projects that began with a good idea are now breathing down my neck because there are deadlines to these things, and what began as a creative outburst is now just Get It Done. I come home exhausted, fried, and that's where the drinking thing turned sour. Sometimes I'll try to get a run in—but did you notice the phrase "get a run in"? Another *get it done*. Even though I do enjoy running, it has become hard to fit it in. Task, not living.

I used to enjoy asking people, "How are you?" Now I avoid the question, because it's an invitation to a conversation I don't have time for, and, it's going to take us into issues I am going to feel obligated to do something about. When a person says, "Not so good," where do we go from there? "Oh, I'm sorry. Well, gotta go." I'm trying not to ask the question, so I can go on with my day and get things done.

Every age has a certain spirit or mood or climate to it. Ours is busyness. We're all running like lemmings from sunup to way past sundown. What's with all the energy drinks? There must be dozens now. RocketFuel. CrankYouUp. Not to mention the coffeehouses on every corner. Why do we need all this caffeine? And why do so many of us now need sleep aids to rest at night? Our grandparents didn't. We thought the age of technology would make life simpler, easier. It has us by the throat. We need to operate at the speed of computers. Seriously, I'm irritated that my e-mail takes four seconds to boot up now, when it used to take ten. I realize I'm not the first to put this down on paper. People have been making this observation for a long time. We are running around like ants do when you kick in their hill, like rats on a wheel, like Carroll's Mad Hatter.

And for some reason, we either believe we can't stop or we don't want to.

Like the prodigal son, we are not going to do a thing about this until we wake one day to realize we are sick of it *and we want a different life*. Till then, the life of not living but getting things done has its benefits. For one, it provides us with an illusion of security—I am tackling life, I am staying on top of things. It's a false security, but we don't believe that. We believe it's our only road to security. Stay on top of things. We might not be so honest as to say, "God doesn't seem particularly involved in taking care of these things for me, so I have to do it." But that is our underlying conviction. After all, if we believed God was going to take care of all that concerns us, we wouldn't kill ourselves trying to hold our world up.

Then there is the wonderful quality of the endless distraction it provides—"purposeful distraction." I don't have to face myself or God or anyone else, because I'm so very busy. And the bonus is, I don't have to feel guilty that I'm not facing myself or God or anyone else, because my busyness is "just the way it is," and by golly, at least I'm showing that I'm a responsible person by getting things done. Thus I can avoid any real disruption while feeling the victim of circumstances beyond my control.

If we really wanted to live differently, we'd show some sign of that in our choices.

So, I am going to turn off this computer and enjoy what is left of the day up here.

Hawks

God has been speaking to me through hawks. No more two-headed roosters. Red-tailed hawks.

A pair of hawks nested at the ranch this summer. I loved to hear their cry. I'd be working on something or other, and suddenly from way up high I'd hear the call of a hawk, and I'd stop to watch them. It was as though they lifted me out of the mundane, lifted me up. Raised not just my gaze but the gaze of my heart. There was also the hawk that God led me to up on the bluff when I thought I was looking for shed antlers. Another hawk swooped overhead as S'mores and I were riding one afternoon out in the sage. He was for me a symbol of God's presence, of his freedom and beauty.

A symbol of My heart, he said.

And then today God gave me a magnificent hawk perched up on the hill above our house. They only come and rest on that snag this time of year, for a week or two, as they migrate through in the fall. I felt God move me after our time of prayer and journaling to go outside, and as I did I felt him move me to *go up*, or *look up*, and there was the biggest hawk I had ever seen. I was afraid that he would not stay long enough for me to get the spotting scope. But he did. And far longer than that. I watched him for about ten minutes. There was a moment when he looked straight down at me, and his eyes almost seemed as if they were the eyes of God. God looking down on me. I asked him what it meant.

My love.

Remember, "The earth is the LORD's, and everything in it" (Psalm 24:1). God is speaking to us all the time. Sometimes he uses words. Other times he uses dreams. And he loves to use the ever-changing, unfolding beauty, drama, and presence of his creation. What was Wordsworth's phrase?

> Thanks to the human heart by which we live,
> Thanks to its tenderness, its joys, and fears,
> To me the meanest flower that blows can give
> Thoughts that do often lie too deep for tears.

(More at walkingwithgod.net)

winter

spring
summer
fall

*finding God in our losses, in
the mundane, and sustaining
our hearts over what can feel like
the long path of obedience*

The Passing of Scout

Our family is grieving.

Our beloved golden retriever, Scout, has died.

It's hard to describe this loss, because you would have to have known Scout and what he meant to our family to understand. This is more than the passing of a pet. Our boys grew up with Scout. He was a part of our family. Not merely because of our affection for him—affection can raise the status of a stuffed rabbit to something special. Scout *was* special. He had a huge heart and a sensitive spirit. He was loyal and true. Always happy to see you, always game for whatever was afoot. He slept in the boys' bedroom. He took walks with Stasi every morning as she said her prayers. He always was at the door when we got home from the day, barking hello, tail wagging.

Scout loved to run through the snow with his nose down in

it. He loved to chase birds. And our ATVs. He'd sometimes come up to S'mores, and when S'mores would bend his tall head down to inspect him, Scout would give him a lick on his nose. He'd want to play ball with you, but he'd never want to give you the ball. And if you were sad, he'd come up to you, gently, lovingly, tail wagging. He'd nuzzle his face close to yours and comfort you. He could tell.

We were sad last Monday night. Really sad. The cancer that had shown up last summer had returned, with a vengeance. The vet gave Scout a month at best. But we could tell he was fading fast. And we didn't want him to suffer. He was having a tough time getting up to go outside to relieve himself. He was yelping in pain in the night. So we talked with the boys Monday night about putting Scout down before the cancer got to the point that we could no longer manage his pain. We all wept. And Scout— who had been unable to get up the entire day on Sunday because of the cancer in his shoulder—got up and came into the family circle, began to come up to each one of us, tail wagging. It was as if he were saying, "It's okay. It's going to be all right." Here he was, comforting his family right to the end.

I cannot tell you how much I wanted to be able to pray and heal Scout. But you have to be *so* careful with your heart and your faith when it comes to healing prayer. It's *so* important to know what God is up to. When the disciples asked Jesus about a man born blind, Jesus said the man had been born blind so that the work of God could be displayed in his life (John 9). And right then and there he healed him. But there were a lot of blind people in Israel at that time whom Jesus *didn't* heal. So a few weeks ago I began to ask, *Jesus, do you want to heal Scout? Is that what you want to do here?* I sensed the answer was *No. Not this time.*

In learning to hear the voice of God, one thing is certain—if you cannot hear a "no," you will have a hard time hearing God at all or believing that what you think you've heard is in fact from God. This is crucial—hearing God requires surrender, giving all things over into his hands. Not abandoning your desires, but yielding them to God. Of course I wanted to hear Jesus say, *Yes, I will heal him.* I wanted to hear that so badly. Then I would have gone after healing prayer like a man on a mission. I would have prayed like Elijah. But I could not do that to my family unless I knew God was fully in it. I didn't want to drag them through that.

But am I just making excuses for my unbelief?

I turned to Romans 4. I'm not quite sure why. But as I read I knew God was speaking to me. "Against all hope, Abraham in hope believed." Yes, that is how I want to live. That's the kind of faith I want to exercise. "Without weakening in his faith, he faced the fact that his body was as good as dead." Right   that's where we are. I'm facing the facts. Apart from a miracle, Scout will soon die. Then came the key verse: "Yet he did not waver through unbelief regarding the promise of God, but was strengthened in his faith and gave glory to God, being fully persuaded that God had power to do what he had promised" (vv. 18–21).

That's the key issue right there—Abraham's faith was based on a clear and specific promise of God. "God had power to do *what he had promised.*"

We did not have God's promise that Scout would live. I asked God long and hard about that.

When it comes to our faith, we have to be careful that our earnest hope and desire don't cause us to claim a promise God has not given. Sometimes well-meaning people will do this on your behalf. Out of their love for you, desperate to offer encouragement, they will come to believe that *their* desire is what God is promising. A lot of mistaken prophetic words come from this desire. They are not the same thing. Of course our friends wanted Scout to live. I wanted him to live. But I did not think we were going to get a miracle this time.

And so I prayed, *Jesus, be with us in this. Help my sons to grieve. Comfort us. I bring the kingdom of God over Scout's passing. I forbid any foul thing to be a part of this. Heal our broken hearts, Lord. Come into this.*

(More at walkingwithgod.net)

God in Our Loss

Scout's passing was the hardest, most beautiful thing we've yet shared with our boys, except for the loss of my dear friend Brent eight years ago. But the boys were very young then, and the grief was largely mine. We were all gathered around Scout. Friends who had come to say their good-byes had excused themselves, to give us the last hour with him alone. The vet was due to come by at five o'clock. And so we sat around Scout on the floor, stroking his soft fur and kissing his nose, telling him we loved him, and weeping. We talked about the things we loved about Scout. He wagged his tail a bit. But mostly we wept. I hated to see my sons grieve so, yet I knew that this was part of their initiation into young manhood. This, too, must be faced. I was grateful they could access their tears.

As the vet walked up the driveway, I told the boys, "It's time to say your good-byes to Scout now. Give him a kiss." And they did, and it broke my heart.

The vet administered putting Scout down right there in our living room. He was such a kind and gracious man. Then he slipped away, to leave us with our grief. Outside, on the hills, the light of the setting sun turned a golden color I've rarely seen. God was so present.

Now, I don't know what you are going to make of this, but I have to tell you the rest of the story. When Scout died, I heard him bark. Not in my memory, not in the past, but in that moment. In the kingdom of God. I thought, *Really? Did I just hear that?* I believe that God preserves the life of animals. After all, the Scripture says the lion will lie down with the lamb. Then there must be at least lions and lambs in the kingdom. Why would God stop there? Many good theologians believe we will see our beloved animals in heaven. But I won't go into a theological debate here. I asked Jesus, *What do dogs do in the kingdom, Lord?* And he said, *They run.* And then I saw Scout, with the eyes of my heart, running with a whole pack of very happy dogs, near the feet of Jesus.

I shared the story with Stasi and the boys, and Blaine said, "Yes, I heard something too. Right after Scout died, Jesus said, '*He won't give me the ball.*'" That was Scout's trademark, to come up to you to play ball, tennis ball already in his mouth, but then he wouldn't give it to you. To hear that from Jesus was more precious to us than I can say.

We buried Scout in the backyard, up the hill in the scrub oak. I'd gone out there the day before to dig the hole. There, lying on the spot I'd chosen, was a small granite stone about the size of your hand, but in the shape of a heart. I kept it, and when we buried Scout I showed it to Stasi and the boys. Another gift from God. He cares about our hearts. Then I placed it on top of the cairn of stones we raised over Scout.

Accept the Grace God Is Giving

I was afraid of Scout's death, afraid of the grief, because when I lost Brent years ago, it was the most excruciating thing I'd ever gone through. I was afraid that this grief would open the door to that one. Sorrow is like that—it seems connected to all the other sorrows in your life. Like opening the door into a room where all your sorrow is stored. But it didn't happen. There are echoes of Brent's death, but this time I feel different. A lot different. It's as if I'm substantially healed. Wow. Healing really does take place.

And there is another thing. When I said good-bye to Scout, I also said, "I'll see you again, boy." It resolved something in my soul. Our losses are not permanent, not when they are in the hands of God. What a difference that makes.

Making the choice to put Scout down is one of the hardest things I have ever done, because I was the one to carry the weight of the decision. I knew the cancer was advancing rapidly. I knew he was growing permanently immobile. But still, to choose the time you will end the life of the family dog is hard. When I prayed Sunday night, I heard God say, *Two days*. We put him down Tuesday. We had two days. As I wrestled with the decision, I also heard God say, *Your hearts*. That was so very kind. It would have been wrenching upon all our hearts to drag this out and let the cancer ravage Scout beyond recognition.

However genuinely hard these things are, they don't have to be brutal and lonely if we will invite God into them.

I've noticed that Jesus is offering comfort and well-being to me today. But I also notice that I have a choice whether to accept them. It almost seems wrong to be feeling okay only days after Scout's death and all that our family went through. Like it somehow diminishes what he meant to me, the sadness of his death, the loss, and especially it somehow diminishes what the others are feeling, because they are not doing well. It's almost a version of survivor's guilt, that thought that says, *I shouldn't be doing well, look at the others.*

Be careful of this. "I ought to feel bad" can quickly become an agreement with feeling bad, and it shouldn't then come as a surprise that pretty soon you start feeling bad. My goodness— accept the grace of God when it comes. It is a gift, and if he's giving it, it must be all right to receive it.

(More at walkingwithgod.net)

The Devil Is an Opportunist

As I wake this morning, Jesus feels near—nearer than he's felt in awhile. And it's so good. I'm so grateful to have him close and to be able to welcome his closeness. Then a heaviness begins to creep over me.

At first it just seems part of the nature of things. *This is just because of Scout—of course you're feeling heavy.* But I don't like the fruit of it. As the heaviness comes in, Jesus' nearness seems to be fading away. Again the thought comes, *Well, of course it's fading away, you are grieving and this is a heavy time.* But no—I want Jesus to be here, and I don't think this is from God. It doesn't feel like God. So I begin to pray against it, and sure enough—it begins to lift. Not immediately, not quickly, but I can sense it beginning to falter in the spiritual realm. Something is here, trying to ride in on the death of Scout, trying to find a window of opportunity here to overshadow us.

We must be aware of this—Satan is an opportunist.

He is always looking for open doors, opportunities, a chink in the armor. He'll seize what might otherwise simply be an event—an argument, an emotion, a loss like this—and he'll use it as an entrée for his lies, deceits, and oppression. I've felt it around someone else's bad news. I'll be doing fine, and then someone will tell me a story of some hardship or loss that a friend is undergoing, and *boom*—a sense of lingering darkness will creep over me, not strong at first, just that sense of, *Right, this is what life is really like—it's hard and unpredictable.* It feels like an assault against my faith. Sure, some of this is my own weirdness and paranoia. But not all of it.

I've seen the reverse as well. I remember driving through a beautiful part of the Southern California coastline a few years back, through a neighborhood of gorgeous homes and luxury cars and massive, immaculate front yards. It felt so good. So hopeful. *You see*, came the thought or impression, *it can be done, life can be good if you are wealthy.* Whether we fall prey to this thinking depends on our worldview, our basic understanding of what's going on down here. From all that I've observed, most folks just let this stuff in, making agreement upon agreement with it all day long, because they don't understand that they have an enemy, or they just don't want to deal with it. And so it has a field day with them.

Here I am, grieving the loss of something very dear to me, and some creep of a spirit is trying to seize the opportunity to take my heart into despair. It would be so easy to go with this. I'm tired and hurting. Do I have to resist this now? If I want to be free of oppression, I do.

Dear friends, you must remember—the world we live in is a world at war.

Why is that so hard to accept? And even if we *do* come to accept it—and few people do—why is it so hard to hang on to that reality every day? What is this propensity, this inclination in us, to ignore the facts? No—that's not strong enough. What is this *insistence* in us to see life the way we want to see it, as opposed to the way it is? Take terrorism as an example. There was an incredible amount of passion and resolve in our national consciousness shortly after the terrorist attacks of 9/11. The attacks woke us up. For a while. Bumper stickers and billboards proclaimed, "We will never forget."

Oh, but we have. We have. We're back to our nice little lives. "Don't disrupt me with a long, drawn-out war against terrorism. I just don't want to deal with it."

On a spiritual level, we've done the same thing, but the consequences are even worse.

Jesus, what is this insistence in us? Why do we insist on forgetting what is painful and hard and reframing our view of the world back to "I want a happy little life"?

I rise up, albeit reluctantly, and begin to pray against this heaviness riding in on my grief. I bring the work of Christ against it, though I feel awkward and dull as I pray. But slowly, the warrior in me is awakening. My eyes fall to the corner of my office, and there, laid against the wall, is a broadsword. It reminds me of reality. We are at war whether I like it or not. It reminds me of what Jesus is like. He is a fierce warrior. My prayers grow more passionate. The heaviness lifts. Once again I am free to bring my heart to God without the enemy fouling my thoughts.

I'm not saying that we cannot allow ourselves to feel what we feel. What I'm warning you about is that when you are in a vulnerable place, realize that you are in a vulnerable place, and remember that all predators look for the vulnerable one in the herd. Once we are in the kingdom that is yet to come, once the world has been restored to all it was meant to be, then we will be able to live without interruption, without assault. Then we can drop our guard. But not until then. Not even in moments of tenderness and sorrow. I know it seems unfair, but the enemy does not play fair. He is an opportunist.

Knowing this will help.

Give Them to Me

One of the most profound surprises that has come about through walking with God has been with regard to people.

People make up a very large part of our lives. We're surrounded by people. We deal with others every day, from the driver in front of us, to the waitress in the café, to the gal in the next office, to those who share our homes. And they are nearly always, one way or another, in some sort of need. Or crisis. Or self-inflicted drama. And one of the great dangers for the person who has begun to desire to please Christ is that we simply let our conscience be our guide in relating to others. We tend to jump in, as opposed to walking with God. Either we give too much or too little, or we offer what is needed, but at the wrong time.

It would be a revealing study to look at the way Jesus relates to people in the Gospel stories. Sometimes he stops midstride to offer a word or a kindness to what seems to me to be a pretty minor character, someone I think I would have ignored. Other times he ducks for cover, dodges an encounter completely (see Luke 5:12–16). He possesses a freedom toward others I find myself longing for.

What would happen if we began to ask Jesus what *he* is saying when it comes to the people in your life?

Jason needs a place to stay. Some of us would simply offer that, without first asking Christ. Some of us would not even consider offering it. But did you ask Christ? Nancy is in need of prayer. My inclination is to jump in. But I stop and ask God, *What would you have me pray?* Sometimes he will then direct my prayers, and I know I am praying far more effectively because I am praying his will, rather than simply praying my thoughts or desires for the person. Or even their requests. Other times he will say, *It's covered. No need to pray here.* And so I am able to let it go. Ben is asking for some time with me. I stop and ask God, *Should I offer here?* Sometimes he will say yes, sometimes no, and sometimes *Not now.*

But more often than any other guidance, what I hear God saying to me when I ask about a person is, *Give them to me.*

This response has been consistently counterintuitive, and utterly refreshing.

I know I'm not alone in this bent I have to carry people. I'll worry about them in the night. *Do my folks have enough money?* I'll get paranoid about what someone thinks of me. *Maybe I shouldn't have said that to Gary, maybe he's mad at me.* I'll find myself having conversations with them even though they are not there. *You know, your daughter wouldn't be so lost if you'd just spend more time with her.* I'll feel as though I am not offering enough. *You ought to call Jim.* At times I think I see what is needed and assume I'm supposed to offer it. *I think I'd better get together with Kyle.*

How do we navigate all our relationships? What is it that currently guides you when it comes to relating to the people in your life?

Our tendency is to go with whatever it is we're feeling. It is not a reliable guide. We run with the speculation, or the worry, guilt, or sense of obligation. Or we give way to the irritation, the malaise, or the desire to write them off. We find ourselves over-committed or entangled in their drama. Then we resent people as a category because we're spent. And the reason?

We never asked God about it.

Again today my battle was to worry about Sally. *Did we do enough? Are we going to lose all that we gained?* But I caught myself obsessing, stopped and asked, *What about Sally, Lord?* And he said, *Give her to me.* Right. Okay. I'm worrying. Let her go. Accepting this is an act of humility—I am not as indispensable as I thought. She needs God more than me. It is an act of faith—that God will come through for her. He'll take care of it. It is an act of release. And I find that when I give people to God, it opens up an amazing amount of space in my life. For him.

The Snare of Speculation

Okay. There's this other thing that's been going on for a long time, and I think I'm finally beginning to see it.

First, there was a conversation Stasi and I had in the kitchen last summer while we were making peanut butter and jelly sandwiches. She was talking about something she'd read on imagination and about what a great gift from God our imagination is. She said, "But the world has assaulted it, through all the dark movies and images that fill our culture. I think we need to be careful what we take in so that we can have a holy imagination."

Huh, I thought. *That makes sense.* But for the life of me, I never thought of my imagination as either holy or unholy. I guess I saw it more as a faculty, like my sense of smell. Anyhow, that was how the Holy Spirit got things going, through a brief observation of Stasi's. It felt weighty. As we stood there in the kitchen wrapping sandwiches in plastic wrap, what she said had that ring to it that is usually God saying, *Pay attention. This is important.* Maybe I felt that way simply because I realized I had never even thought about it before. And holy smokes, here was an entire region of my life I'd never sanctified.

So, as I left the kitchen to carry on with the day, I prayed, *Jesus, I give you my imagination.* (Remember—now is the time. Go with it. You don't know when a subject will come up again.) *Sanctify my imagination.* That's about all I knew to do at the time.

Now, I thought the sanctification would come through a time of prayer, cleansing of old memories, something like that. But here is what unfolded. I began to notice that my imagination just takes off on a whim with all sorts of scenarios during the course of a day. Stasi mentions that someone's child has left the faith, and I immediately go to *Wow, that could happen to us. Is it Blaine? Sam? Luke?* I start imagining the possibilities. We have a bad month financially, and I run with the thought, *We're going to end up living under a bridge.* The truck makes a thumping noise when I start it, and my imagination jumps to *The engine's going. I'd better sell it before it implodes.* I can already see it up on blocks in front of the house.

Another word for this is *speculation.* Entertaining possibilities, such as, *I could get mouth cancer* or *This plane could go down.* My imagination has all the restraint of a wild horse.

The speculation thing was happening a lot in my relationships. Leigh misses one of our church meetings, and I think, *She's drifting away. We're losing her. Any day now she'll be gone.* All she was doing was visiting a friend. Morgan sends an e-mail, "Can I talk to you?" and I think, *He's going down. Something's gone wrong. It's probably a meltdown in the events department.* Turns out he had a question about a book. Craig skips a staff meeting, and I jump to *What—we're not a priority? He thinks he can just come and go as he pleases? What an arrogant way to live.* He had a doctor's appointment. This speculation is devastating to relationships, and mine was running rampant.

But the thing that really began to kill me was speculation and an entertaining of dark possibilities regarding my own holiness.

In an effort to make sure that I was pure before God, that things were right between us, I would race through my heart and conscience looking for anything that might be out of whack, anything that might displease God. A kind of soul searching, if you will, but done in a spirit of *I bet there is something here that's not right.* Now, this can be motivated by an earnest desire to be clean before God. I think it's appropriate to be aware of the ways we may have turned our hearts from him over the course of a day. But what I am describing is different than a gentle openness to the prompting of the Holy Spirit in matters of confession and repentance.

It's a form of hypochondria.

If you are constantly giving your physical well-being a thorough going-over, looking for any sign of distress, guess what— you'll find something to obsess about. You'll find something, and however small or slight it may be, you'll quickly blow it out of proportion. *That tickle in my throat—I'm coming down with strep.*

That pain in my wrist—did I overdo it yesterday? Set back my healing because of it?

If you begin to introduce uncertainty into your soul with the search for something wrong there, under the conviction *something's wrong*, well guess what—you'll soon find yourself in distress, because something *is* wrong. What's wrong is that you're no longer trusting God. You've moved out of the restful posture of faith and assurance, and that *is* wrong (unbelief and mistrust are wrong). The soul begins to manifest the signs of *something's wrong*. But the sad irony is that we don't notice what's really wrong—the fact that we're operating out of fear and mistrust—because we're looking for something else, some sin we're afraid we've committed, some turn of the heart toward an idol. And all the while what's wrong is this mistrust that got us looking in the first place.

This obsessing is no different than common worry. Whether there is something to worry about in this or that relationship, event, or plan, you'll find that if you begin to entertain worry, you'll soon find yourself in a *state* of worry, regardless of the situation. And once you're in a state of worry, you'll notice that your imagination turns all evidence into further cause for worry. You wake in the night. You begin to wonder, *Did I hear something?* If you are in any way vulnerable to a fear of things that go bump in the night, then guess what you'll begin to hear, sitting there in the dark with the blankets pulled up around you, straining to identify what woke you. Things will start to go bump in the night. This is the cycle of which I speak.

You shall know them by their fruit. My obsessing has brought only distress, and Satan the opportunist has used it time and time again. I have to bring my imagination under the rule of God, under the guidance of the Holy Spirit. It is unfettered, reckless, unchecked—and therefore unsanctified. "We take captive every thought to make it obedient to Christ" (2 Corinthians 10:5). That is exactly what I have to do. I have to lasso this thing.

No more speculation. It's so utterly godless. And it has absolutely wrung me out, filled my soul with distress. It's taking some time and conscious effort to bring under control an imagination that has never been asked to accept the bridle, but it's coming around. And the fruit is peace and a much more tranquil inner life.

I sanctify my imagination to the Lordship of Jesus Christ.

It Will Come Around

Last week Gary, Craig, and I had two days together, sitting around with our feet up, cup of coffee in hand, talking about the future of our ministry. When we began to form the ministry that has become Ransomed Heart, Craig set before us the idea that we operate in a trinitarian leadership, a shared approach to ruling the kingdom. No man has ultimate say. No one gets to be the absolute ruler. The three of us lead together. And so, over time, we have developed a way of walking and leading as a team. At the center of that is listening to the voice of God. Together. I can't tell you how much tension has been relieved, how many meetings have become unnecessary, and how many collisions have been avoided because the three of us stopped to listen. Together.

I didn't want to go to Canada for an event in 2006. Gary felt we should. So did Craig. There's no talking your way through impasses like this, or, if you can, it takes hours and hours. We stopped and asked God. *Go,* he said. And that was that. Asking God for his will is a great preserver of relationships, because you don't have all those lingering feelings of *I wish Craig hadn't dug in his heels on that one.* Or the festering undercurrent of *I was right. Why won't Gary admit that?* Or the pressure to see everything eye to eye. All that is required is for each man to listen to God.

Pause. Listening to God would be a tremendous source of guidance and relief for the leaders of churches, ministries, and businesses if they would adopt this approach in their day-to-day decision making. Ask God. Listen for his voice. Together. Surrender to what you hear. Think of all the foolish things that would be avoided, and all the noble things God has for us to embrace. It's an act of humility, really, by which we admit we haven't the smarts to run this thing and we need the counsel of God. In the small things as much as the big ones.

(More at walkingwithgod.net)

Anyhow, last week was but one of many occasions when we sat down with a blank page before us and prayed and talked and let God lead, both in our relationships and with regard to plans for the ministry. Perhaps the best part of our meanderings was to hear my friends talk about the things that God had been bringing up in their lives and urging them to deal with. I felt relieved.

You see, whenever we live in relationship, whenever we simply live in *proximity* to other people, sooner or later we will run up against their issues—the unhealed or unholy parts of their personalities. Just as they will run into ours. Living in community is like a pack of porcupines sharing the same den. We will get stuck. And the question presses in, *What do I do with what I see?* I'm not talking about getting jostled by somebody's rough edges on a given day. Rather, what will you do when you are continually hitting up against patterns in someone's life that are hurting them and others (including you) and also hurting the work God has given them to do? Should you bring it up?

Ask God.

For you must beware—the very thing you want to speak to is booby-trapped. Just as its counterpart is in you. Booby-trapped in the sense that you can't just walk in and make your observation and expect things to go swimmingly. Of course, there's the usual defensiveness and anger we often meet when lifting the lid on someone's life. But the booby trap is more than that. Quite often the issue is entangled with deep wounds in that person's heart, and what bugs you is, for them, a long-developed and carefully honed defense mechanism. You go poking around in there and the booby trap goes off—shame, anger, withdrawal, self-contempt. And if the enemy has a stronghold there, you'll just wake the guard dog and it will turn on both of you.

This is going to take humility and submission.

Walk with God. *When do I bring this up, Lord? What do I say?* Then wait for the go-ahead, even if it means months or years. It will take real restraint. Genuine holiness. But what you can rest assured in is this—the issue will come around again. This isn't the only chance you'll have. Pray as soon as you encounter it, but be willing to let it go, no matter how tweaked you are, if that's what God says to do. It will come around again. The beauty of what happened this last week with Gary and Craig is that I waited—though Lord knows there were times I didn't want to—and here God had been at work and handled the issue much better than I ever could have.

"There is a time for everything," Solomon reminds us, "and

a season for every activity under heaven . . . a time to be silent and a time to speak" (Ecclesiastes 3:1, 7). I'm just not wise enough or compassionate enough or brave enough or gentle enough to always discern if this is the time to venture into someone else's life. So I ask God. And wait. It will come around.

(More at walkingwithgod.net)

In You

I just remembered something God said to me on a kayak trip last month. Good grief—I nearly forgot about it entirely.

A few of us dads had been looking for something special to do with our sons. I'd heard about a sea kayaking trip some young men I know lead each year down in Mexico. I've been wanting to get my sons around these guys because they are the kind of young men I know my boys would look up to—they are adventurers, they love the same kind of music, and they are really cool. *And*—this is Dad's angle—they love Jesus. So, part of my plot was to get in on the kayak trip simply for my boys' sake, a father's ploy to urge them toward a deeper walk with Christ. And, to be honest, part of me just wanted to go to Mexico.

The trip was on, then it was off. It was on, then off. Several guys bailed. I was tempted to as well. Who had time for this? Then I realized that this joy was worth fighting for.

We drove about six hours south of the US border at Nogales, down to an uncharted dirt road leading to the Sea of Cortez, where we put in for a four-day paddle. The desert there surprised me with its lush beauty—saguaro cactus everywhere, ocotillo, mesquite, cholla—a green and living desert. And the beaches were deserted, which was just what we were hoping for. We'd paddle along the coast in the morning, and after we'd make camp each afternoon, we'd wander around looking for shells, digging clams, or playing a pickup game of some sort. Baseball that turned into dodgeball that turned into throw somebody in the water.

And each day, we'd put a question on the table for each of us to take to God in some time alone on the beach. On the last day of the trip, the question was *How am I doing, God? How do I think I'm doing, and how do you think I'm doing?* I suggested the question for the day, because I sensed that God wanted to speak into that great disparity between how we see ourselves and how he sees us. (Wouldn't *that* be good to hear?) By asking him first to reveal what we've been believing, it helps to expose the lies and pressures and accusations we've been living under without even knowing it, and makes the second question all the more poignant. Once what you have been believing is exposed, it is very powerful to hear from God the antidote to that, to hear what is true.

I wandered off down the beach to get a little space so I could be fully present to God. Plopped down on the sand. Started to get distracted by all the driftwood and stones around me. *Wow, how long has that been lying here, do you suppose? I wonder if that rock would make a good necklace?* Caught myself, and remembered I had questions to ask of God. Settled myself. Quieted the internal chatter. Then asked, *How do I think I'm doing God? How do you think I'm doing?* And this is what I heard: *Just barely.* And then, *In you.* Both phrases came totally unsuspected, seemed to come out of the blue. But, oh, how utterly precise they were.

Just barely. Geez. I had no idea that this is what I'd fallen to believing about myself and my life, my walk with God. But having words put to it for me, my soul knew at once that it was true—that is, knew this was exactly what I was convinced about myself. I felt I was just barely walking with God. Just barely getting by as a father. Just barely living as a good man. Just barely. Yep, that's what seemed true to me. That's sure how I feel most days, and it had crept in to become my norm without me really being aware of it. Till now.

The *In you* was even more surprising and intriguing. After hearing *Just barely,* I sort of expected God to say something reassuring (for he is so kind), something aimed directly at *Just barely,* maybe something like *You're doing great* or *I'm proud of you.* I'd have settled for *Naw, that's not true.* But those words did not come. Instead, he said, *In you.*

"In you"? What's that supposed to mean? Somewhere way down in the depths of me, I could sense a comfort and assurance in the phrase, sensed it was speaking to some deep need. But for the life of me, in the moment, I didn't get it. "In you"? What's in me? I sat for a while digging my feet in the sand in a sort of agitated way, sitting with both phrases and asking God what the second one meant. (Ask the next question.) What's *in me?*

I am in you.

Busted. That's how I felt. Totally busted.

His line of approach caught me off guard and took me straight to the heart of the issue. Here's how it worked. I had been trying really hard to be a good dad. To live a life of genuine integrity. To walk with God. Truth is, I was worn out from trying so hard and was feeling like I was just barely making it. When he said, *I am in you,* suddenly, with that clarity only the Holy Spirit gives, it was clear to me that it is *his* life in me that is supposed to be my hope of being a good dad and a good man, of walking well with him. All in a moment I was aware that my hopes had somehow shifted to my integrity and my ability to self-discipline and self-motivate. To endure. To make it happen.

In you. I looked down the shore and saw that our time was up, saw the guys beginning to gather back at camp, and I was so undone by what God had said that I knew I couldn't tie this up with a neat little bow, so I just prayed something like this: *You're right. I receive it. Forgive me. Stay with me on this.* (I pray, *Stay with me on this,* when I know it's going to be some time before I have a chance to get back to whatever it is God has just revealed.) That was the last day of our trip. The next morning we woke before dawn, packed without breakfast or even a cup of coffee, and began to paddle back in the dark. Then we had a long drive to the States to face the pile of stuff to do that had grown since we were gone.

But I wrote the two phrases down on a piece of paper—"Just barely," "In you"—and left it lying on my desk in hopes that at some point down the road I would see it, remember, and have the time to return to the gift God had given.

Two weeks later I'm reading some Scripture in the morning. I look down, and my Bible is open to Colossians 1:27, which is underlined. (When did I do that? What clarity did I have way back when that led me to underline this verse? I have no idea.) Here is the context of Paul's letter:

> This is the gospel that you heard and that has been proclaimed to every creature under heaven, and of which I, Paul, have become a servant. . . . I have become its servant by the commission God gave me to present to you the word of God in its fullness—the mystery that has been kept hidden for ages and generations, but is now disclosed to the saints. To them God

has chosen to make known among the Gentiles the glorious riches of this mystery, which is Christ in you, the hope of glory. (Colossians 1:23, 25–27)

"In you."

Wow. My soul swells with satisfaction.

God brought me back to this. He stayed with me. "In you." This is just so reassuring. He stays with us on the things he is trying to speak to us about. Especially when we ask him to.

The Power of the Right Word

When Jesus said to me on the beach in Mexico, *Just barely*, I was first struck by the brevity of the phrase. And by the freshness of it. I hadn't been using it. But it was right on. A bull's-eye. A perfect phrase for what I was believing but didn't know I was believing, and it also had the quality of haunting me. It unnerved me. I didn't like it. But I knew immediately that it was true. And it was the kind of expression I could hang on to without a pen or journal nearby, could hang on to for several days in the wilderness until I did get to a place where I could write it down and give it some more thought.

Wasn't that both kind and effective?

That's why I have found it so rich to ask Jesus what he is saying to us. For he knows the very words we need to hear. What he will say to me is exactly what my heart needs to hear, will be the very words that best convey his meaning to my heart with greatest precision. He may speak to you on the very same subject, but he will choose the words that are best for you to get his meaning and spirit across. For he knows us, and he wants us to understand not just what he says but what he *means* and the spirit of his meaning.

Language is important, because words and phrases are vehicles of meaning, and *meaning* is what we are after. Some words are more accurate than others. Some words mislead, because the meaning we have attached to them is different than the meaning the user attaches to them. For example, Luke comes home from lacrosse practice the other night, and I asked him how it went.

"I totally wrecked," he said.

"Oh no," I replied. "Are you all right?"

He looked at me like I was an idiot, a way-out-of-touch grown-up. "Wrecked means awesome, Dad. It means I trashed the other team."

"Oh," I said. "Great. Way to go." And I filed the word away in my Luke lexicon. *Wrecked.* Got it.

The generation gap in language is why we need new translations of the Scriptures. What was deep and emotionally meaningful to our forefathers may seem weird or obtuse or may even mean the opposite to us. For example, the Scriptures invite us to an intimacy with God as a secure son or daughter experiences with a father who adores him or her. "For you did not receive a spirit that makes you a slave again to fear, but you received the Spirit of sonship. And by him we cry, *"Abba,* Father" (Romans 8:15). *Abba* means "daddy," a term of endearment. Now, I realize that many people have yet to find that intimacy with God. And language might be part of the problem.

Do you know anyone who addresses their father with Thee and Thou? If you overheard someone talking to his father that way, what would you assume about their relationship? Friends of ours who were required to call their father "Sir" growing up felt a certain distance from him. Respect, but not intimacy. Especially when compared with other homes and families who called their father daddy.

Now, I know, I know—the argument of those who love the Thee and Thou lexicon of church language goes something like this: "We must learn reverence and respect for God who is most high. Casual language teaches people to be casual with God."

But what about the parable of the prodigal son? And what about "*Abba*, Father"? When we insist on clinging to certain phrases because we like their religious tone, we can actually end up embracing a very different, even *opposite* meaning of the gospel than the Scriptures themselves intend.

> How have we learned Christ? It ought to be a startling thought, that we may have learned him wrong. That must be far worse than not to have learned him at all: his place is occupied by a false Christ, hard to exorcise! The point is, whether we have learned Christ as he taught himself, or as men have taught him who thought they understood, but did not understand him. . . . The Christian religion, throughout its history, has been open to more corrupt misrepresentation. Have we learned Christ in false statements and corrupted lessons about him, or have we learned *himself*? (George MacDonald, *The Truth in Jesus*)

It is very helpful to realize that words and phrases carry a certain meaning and spirit to us, because certain phrases open up our hearts to the meaning God intended, and other words and phrases close our hearts to his meaning. I noticed during my years of counseling how a simple turn of a phrase or different word choices would suddenly open up someone's heart, and they would begin weeping over an issue we had spent months talking about. With the right choice of words, the truth would finally strike home. Sink in. Reach them where it mattered.

Peter said of Jesus that he had the words of eternal life (John 6:68). This is a good test. Ask, *Does what I have heard in fact bring life?* If not, perhaps you have not yet found the meaning of Jesus, not yet found the words that convey the spirit of his teaching to your heart in particular. I am not saying that we are always going to like what Jesus said, or is saying, to us. Surely his words sometimes bring conviction and cut to the quick. But even then, when the conviction of God comes, is there not life in it? To be known, to be found out, is in some sense a great relief—if the spirit in which it comes also offers to us, as God is constantly offering, a way out through repentance and forgiveness.

Just barely and *In you* were exactly what I needed to hear. The words pierced, exposed, comforted, and intrigued me to seek more, all at the same time. That is the beauty of asking God what his word to us is, personally. And when we come up against a religious word or phrase in our reading or in some religious context, no matter how precious it may be to a certain translation or body of believers, if it conveys a meaning and a spirit other than the meaning and spirit of Jesus Christ, then we must reject it. We do not worship language, we worship the *living* God, who assures us that his word to us is life (John 6:63).

Things That Go Bump in the Night

I was awakened at 4:30 this morning. Something reached into the deep bliss of my REM sleep and yanked me clean out of it.

Howling winds were playing havoc with the Christmas wreaths hung outside our bedroom window. Metal, greenery, and pinecones scratching back and forth across glass, *screee-ee-ee, screee-ee-ee.* Like something out of a Hitchcock movie. Dang. I needed sleep really badly. Even took a sleep aid to try and knock myself out for seven or eight hours. But that's over. *Screee-ee-ee.* I noticed a subtle agreement when first I woke: *Well, there goes the night. I'm hosed. I can't go back to sleep.* (The agreement was reinforced by the fact that Craig has been waking up at 4:30 for some time now.) But no—I wasn't just going to surrender my sleep like that. I rejected the agreement, prayed some, and did eventually fall back into unconsciousness for another forty minutes or so.

A couple of hours later, getting into the morning here in my office, I'm sitting down to write, and the thought again passes through, *You're probably going to start waking up at 4:30 a lot. It just comes with getting older. And it's not so bad really. You can live with that.* Geez, flippin' Louise. These guys just don't quit. If I begin to make that agreement, guess what's going to happen—I *am* going to start to wake at 4:30 consistently, and I'm going to accept it as just part of growing older and never see the thief behind my stolen rest.

How many things do we surrender with these subtle agreements?

I used to be such a good sleeper. It was a forte of mine. I'd lay my head on the pillow and be down for the count. Immovable till the alarm went off. Sigh. Those were the days. Our sleep has been assaulted for the past eight years—ever since we started Ransomed Heart. At first it began with my body jerking and twitching for no reason at all. The sensation was like when you have those dreams of falling, or missing the last step of the stairs, and you pull up to compensate and your body actually does yank you right out of the dream. Sort of like that. It would startle me awake, and once awake, I'd find it nearly impossible to fall back to sleep.

The jerking and twitching thing stopped once we prayed about it. Well, after a couple *months* of prayer. But other forms of assault came in—like not being able to fall asleep even though we were utterly exhausted, or waking in the night with a deep fear or dread in the room, or nightmares, or this waking in the very early morning (that's a subtle one, because you did sleep and it's early morning and maybe you're just going to have to start the day early). *But*, you shall know them by their fruit. The fruit was exhaustion, discouragement, and diminishing joy and enthusiasm for everything else in life. Sounds like the thief to me.

When you have sleep problems, folks begin to make suggestions. "When the enemy wakes you up, defeat his purposes by getting up and reading your Bible. He won't like that, and he'll stop waking you up." Tried it. I just wound up exhausted, vaguely familiar with the book of Joshua, and weary for anything else during the day. "Listen to this song—it's a really sweet song about Jesus covering you in your sleep." Tried it. Wasn't strong enough medicine for the demons we were dealing with. Lovely song, lovely thought, totally ineffective.

We began to do some research on spiritual warfare and began experimenting with prayer. I found some encouragement in the fact that Paul listed sleeplessness as one of the things he had to face: "Rather, as servants of God we commend ourselves in every way: in great endurance; in troubles, hardships and distresses; in beatings, imprisonments and riots; in hard work, sleepless nights and hunger" (2 Corinthians 6:4–5). It's not exactly a list of things you'd like for Christmas, but it helps to know you're not blowing it somehow when this stuff happens.

Pause. That feeling nearly always hits me when I've come under one form of spiritual assault or another—I feel like I've blown it. It's because of me. I've done something to bring it on. It's just like the enemy to do this, add insult to injury. Kick you when you're down. Hammer you and blame you for it. Anyhow, to see sleeplessness listed among Paul's battles actually brought assurance. Okay. This is just part of the deal.

Now deal with it.

Stasi and I have to pray for about twenty minutes before we go to bed, or we don't stand a good chance of seeing never-never land. But it's really made a difference. We can sleep now, praise God. Not all the time, not like back in the good old days of hitting the pillow without even an "Our Father" and sleeping hard all night. Some nights our bedtime prayers are just round one (remember Elijah), and we have to pray again later in the night.

The prayer looks something like this: First, I find I need to be restored and renewed in Jesus at the end of the day. I wish it weren't so, but I haven't yet learned to abide in Christ all day long, every day. I wander. I think most of us do. I strive, I indulge, I forget. I get all wrung out. It's the whole "remain in me" thing. I haven't been able to pull it off day after day. So I begin at bedtime by offering myself to Jesus once more, coming back under his authority and covering. The only safe place to be. And I cleanse and sanctify my home as well. It's an act of consecration. Rededication.

My dear Lord Jesus, I come to you now to be restored in you, to be renewed in you, to receive your love and life, to take refuge in you. I honor you as my Sovereign, and I surrender every aspect of my life totally and completely to you. I give you my body, soul, and

spirit; my heart, mind, and will. I cover myself with your blood,
and I ask your Holy Spirit to restore my union with you, renew
me in you, and lead me in this time of prayer. [Sometimes I add
"my imagination" or "my sexuality" if I sense consecration is
needed there. And because we have children, we consecrate our
sons as well].

I bring the kingdom of God and the authority of the Lord
Jesus Christ over my home, my bedroom, my sleeping, all through
the hours of this night and the new day. I bring the full work of the
Lord Jesus Christ throughout my home tonight—the atmosphere in
every room, over every object and furnishing, all media, and the
very structure of my home.

Then I bring the full work of Christ between me and everyone I've been with during the day. Paul said that through "the
cross of our Lord Jesus Christ . . . the world has been crucified
to me, and I to the world" (Galatians 6:14). It's good to announce
that, apply it at the end of each day. This blanket protection is
good because of that computer virus thing—their warfare may
have jumped on you without you even recognizing it yet, and
you don't want all their stuff hanging around your bedroom
tonight.

And in the authority of Jesus Christ I bring the full work of Jesus
Christ between me and all people now—their spirits, souls, and
bodies, their sin and warfare. [I name those people now.]

As I pray this I listen to God, letting him bring people to
mind, for I may need to bring the cross of Christ between us
specifically. I'll completely forget that only four hours ago I was

counseling someone battling suicidal thoughts and depression, and I sure don't want that stuff around here tonight. Then I bring the work of Christ against all witchcraft. Pagan rites and rituals are back in force these days, and there's a lot of witchcraft raised against the church—curses, rituals, stuff like that. The culture we live in now is like Egypt or Babylon of the Old Testament. Bizarre is in. Demonic is in. But it's nothing to get freaked out about— it's no different than what any modern missionary in Brazil or Uganda has to deal with.

> *I command the judgment of the Lord Jesus Christ on every foul power and black art. I bring the cross and the blood of Christ, I bring his resurrection and life, his authority rule, and dominion against every hex, vex, and incantation. Against every spell, all rituals, and all ritual devices, all satanic rituals and satanic ritual devices. Against every vow, dedication, and sacrifice. Against every word, every judgment, and every curse. I send it all to the abyss in the authority of the Lord Jesus Christ and in his name.*

Next, I bring the work of Christ against all foul spirits, naming those I know have been assaulting me. Every one of us has a list of the usual suspects, if we'll think about it. For some it's fear, discouragement, and depression. For others it's more like anger, rage, and lust. For the rest of us, the list grows pretty long and begins to sound like a menagerie of all that hell has to offer. Naming them has proven important. Adam was given authority to name things, and in doing so he exercised a sort of authority over them. The principle holds here. You're dealing with twisted beings who have no intention of yielding. The more specific and direct you can be, the better (see Mark 5:1–13).

I now bring the authority of the Lord Jesus Christ and the fullness of his work against Satan and his kingdom. I bring the cross, resurrection, and ascension of Jesus Christ against every foul and unclean spirit—every ruler, power, authority, and spiritual force of wickedness [Ephesians 6:12]. *I command all foul and unclean spirits bound from my home and from my household* [remember, "bind the strong man"], *together with all their underlings, backups, and replacements, in the authority of the Lord Jesus Christ and in his name.*

Again, this is just the framework for the prayer. As I pray I listen to Jesus, because what assailed me yesterday may have been replaced by something else today. I end by bringing the kingdom of God and the authority of Jesus Christ over my home and family and over all the hours of the night. I ask God to send his angels to protect us.

I announce the kingdom of God over my home and my house this night. I summon the angels of the Lord Jesus Christ and ask them to build a shield of protection around me and my home [Hebrews 1:14]. *I ask your Spirit to fill my home with your presence and to go forth and raise up prayer and intercession for me this night. All this I pray in the mighty name of the Lord Jesus Christ, to his glory. Amen.*

This is the short version, the general outline. I offer it with the hope that it will be a help to you. I fear you're going to think I'm nuts.

Yes, it's a hassle to do this. Especially when you get home late and all you want to do is fall into bed. Yes, you won't want to do it every night for months and years. I have friends who struggle with their sleep but won't pray about it. I understand. There are lots of nights I wish I didn't have to. But it's worth it. For one, you'll get a good part of your sleep back. Maybe all of it. But for another, it will make you holy. To come to Christ and realign yourself with him at the end of your day when you *are* utterly spent and *don't* want to pray has a deeply sanctifying effect.

(More at walkingwithgod.net)

Aching

I noticed that I'm daydreaming a lot lately.

I'm thinking about getting a new pair of sunglasses, negotiating the next contract with my publisher, buying a tractor, or maybe I'll buy myself a pair of really cool ski goggles like Sam and Blaine got for Christmas. It feels as if I'm almost reaching out for something. I am not a shopper by nature. What in the world am I reaching for? Did losing alcohol allow this to surface? The whole joy in a bottle thing? To numb some pain in my soul? Some emptiness? Isn't that why most people drink—to try and get a little joy and numb the pain without ever admitting that they're doing either? How much of this has to do with not having anything to look forward to?

So what is going on with my heart, Lord Jesus? I feel sad.

I know I was made for Eden. I know I don't have anything close to that every day. Most of the time I just use busyness to cover up all the longings in my soul, create some distance between me and them. But then I notice I am daydreaming about stuff. It comes back to, what is there for *my* heart?

Jesus, come to my heart in this. Be my companion. My constant companion.

Do I love my life? Do I even want to answer that question?

Tears are here now. But I feel like I'm skirting around the edge of some mountainous issue. I feel as if the way I live is just "keeping life from going bad." Push hard, get it done, come through, because no one else will. Why, as I'm writing this, isn't my heart engaged? I don't think I've found the right words yet. It feels like I'm getting warm, but not hot.

Then there is the warfare. I've wondered before what the toll of daily assault is doing to me. What do soldiers in a long, drawn-out war like Vietnam feel? There are many days and hours when just to be free from oppression or temptation or testing or some physical assault seems good. I don't think about having joy so much as just wanting to get free from pain or assault. I know this plays a *huge* part, more than I realize, because I know I underestimate my willingness to endure.

Okay. That word rings. Hurts, even. *Endure.* I underestimate my willingness to endure. This feels like the source of my ache. I put my head in my hands for a long time. This is the one quality I think I like most about myself, feel most noble about—my willingness to endure. And yet I think it has become something other than noble. Perhaps even something destructive.

Jesus, come in here. Come in here. What do you want to say to me here, in this?

Long silence. Am I even able to hear God in this, about this? Is it too big, too close?

This whole *endure* thing is definitely it, though. I know I'm onto something huge here. There is little room for joy in my life when I'm living like this. There isn't much room for joy in Endure. I'm trying to sort this out. Where did it come from? Is it sin? Woundedness? How deep does this run in me? I think there is a lot of unbelief behind Endure, like my conviction that no one else is going to come through, so I have to. It also feels like Samson's downfall—we find a quality or a strength that helps us get through life, and we make it our idol, put all our trust and hope in it. For some it's their intelligence. For others, their ability to make people happy. For me, it has been my willingness to endure.

But once we make this strength or quality an idol and turn to it for security, it becomes our blind spot—the thing we don't want anyone to look at or tamper with. Not even God. Eventually it becomes our ruin.

Jesus, I don't want to say that this is the unapproachable subject. You can speak to me here, about this. I want you to. I invite you to.

Motive

Let's come back to something very basic to our pursuit of God and the transformation he is always after in our lives—everything we do has a reason behind it, a motive.

Within the Christian community we tend to focus on behavior, and that is right and that is wrong. Of course what we do matters. It matters how you treat people. It matters whether you lie or steal or commit adultery. Our actions have enormous consequences to them. However, according to Jesus, holiness is a matter of the heart. This is the gist of his famous Sermon on the Mount. Jesus asks, "Why do you pray—to be seen as holy? Why do you give—to be seen as generous? Why do you fast—to impress others?"

> "Be careful not to do your 'acts of righteousness' before men, to be seen by them. If you do, you will have no reward from

your Father in heaven. So when you give to the needy, do not announce it with trumpets, as the hypocrites do. . . .

"And when you pray, do not be like the hypocrites, for they love to pray standing in the synagogues and on the street corners to be seen by men. . . .

"When you fast, do not look somber as the hypocrites do, for they disfigure their faces to show men they are fasting. I tell you the truth, they have received their reward in full. But when you fast, put oil on your head and wash your face, so that it will not be obvious to men that you are fasting, but only to your Father, who is unseen; and your Father, who sees what is done in secret, will reward you." (Matthew 6:1–2, 5, 16–18)

Jesus is moving the whole question of genuine goodness from the external to the internal. He is taking us back to motive. If we will follow him in this, it will open up fields of goodness for us.

If we'll be honest about what compels us.

I noticed that at the retreats we do, I am careful to be kind and attentive to people. Why is that? It could be love. But might it also be that I want to be *seen* as kind and attentive? I spent a lot of time working on this book. Why? Is it to bring the truth as best I can—or to impress you, to be thought well of, to avoid embarrassment?

You have something to say to a friend or coworker, and you choose e-mail. Why? Is it because it will help them understand you better or because it is easier to fire a shot from a distance?

We're faithful to attend church. Why? Is it because we are really worshiping God or because we know people will talk if we don't? We hate confrontation, and we never speak up in a meeting. Why? Is it humility, or is it so that everyone will like us? We want our children to behave in public. Why? Might it have something to do with the fact that they are a reflection on us? How about what we choose to wear—is it because we like it? Or because it will cause others to think we're rugged or really cool or sexy, or because we desperately want to fit in and we're scared to death of what others will say?

Everything we do has a motive behind it.

Now, what most people don't realize is that what we call our personality has some very deep and profound motives behind it as well. Call it your approach to life. Have you ever asked yourself what's behind it? As I've already shared, I can be a very driven man. Part of that comes out of some childhood wounds. I found myself on my own. But part of it comes out of my sinful response to those wounds—my resolution to make it on my own. I won't need anyone. Not even God.

Some of you are always friendly. (I can't seem to pull that one off.) Is it just your natural buoyancy—or is your personality driven by a fear of rejection? You say you're not an organized person—now that may be true, but how does that work for you? How convenient it is to put the burden of organization on others.

I know men who say they're just not comfortable in the outdoors—they don't go for all that outdoor stuff. Now, that may be a matter of preference—but how does that work for them? Perhaps they don't want to be tested and exposed. Perhaps it's fear of not really being a man that keeps them at home.

I hear women say, "I'm not into all that women's stuff, dresses and beauty and all that." It might be true. It might be that they're more of the tomboy sort. Then again, how does that work for them? Are they able to avoid facing issues of insecurity, doubts about their femininity?

We all have an approach to life, and we all think it's perfectly justified. But would you be willing to have a look?

Most of the folks I know have never even considered that their *personality* has a motive behind it, and that the motive might not be noble. "It's just the way I am." Maybe. But permit me to disrupt. Scripture says that "everything that does not come from faith is sin" (Romans 14:23). You might say, "I just don't like confrontation," when in fact what's really going on is that you are terrified of what might happen to the relationship if you confront the person. Your refusal to confront is based on fear. And unbelief. And whatever is not from faith is sin.

Now, I am not saying this to usher in waves of self-reproach and despair. You may be thinking, *I'm a disaster. I'm a nightmare of twisted motives. Who even knows all that's going on down in there? Whatever is not from faith is sin??? My whole approach to life is suspect.* Probably. Take a number. It's true for the rest of us as well. That's okay. You are forgiven. God has been well aware of your motives for years, and still he has been right there with you. Isn't he gracious and patient? But now you have the opportunity to be transformed in some really genuine ways.

Our motives are an essential category to consider when we are learning to walk with God. As I'm listening for his voice, I'm also watching my own motives. What's going on inside? Am I willing to hear *anything* God wants to say? As I yield and repent and give over even my personality to God, the lines of communication are opened up. We grow closer.

Or better, I draw nearer.

Healing the Past

I thought the invitation I gave God into my motives, and into their connection to the ache in my heart, was going to take me in the direction of some hard soul searching, which I figured would lead to another round of repentance.

Instead, God surprised me through healing.

Last night the gang threw a party for me, to celebrate the release of a book I'd written. Back to the book party. As the afternoon wore on and the hour of the party approached, I found myself growing more and more nervous. I don't do parties for me well. I don't like being the center of attention. But there is more—it feels like there is such an ache for joy I can take into a party, hoping for that transcendent moment. Then I end up drinking because it's not there.

I felt that I needed a time of prayer beforehand to prepare my heart. I didn't want to be ruled by my fear. I wanted to be in a good place to go. What began as a simple, *Jesus, help me with this evening, give me something to hold on to*, turned into a longer time of prayer about my posture toward parties in general. Back in high school I was a big-time partier and ran with a crowd of heavy partiers. We were known for our party expertise. Anyhow, I have some really mixed memories from back then. We were, all of us, chasing that transcendent moment. We knew there had to be more to life than Mr. Blagstop's chemistry class, and we were desperate to find it. We looked in some pretty dark places.

As I was praying about all this, I began to ask forgiveness for the things that happened during those years. I wasn't repenting of my search for joy, but of the places I let it take me. I found myself then praying against despair as the deeper issue. Let me explain.

I didn't grow up in a Christian home. My dad went through some hard years of unemployment and fell to drinking. My mom went back to work. By the time I was in high school, my family had fallen apart. As I was praying about those years, I began to see how the collapse at home sent me on this search. It's as if, having made an agreement with despair, I turned to those parties to get high and make out with girls, grasping to fill the ache with something.

I sensed Jesus saying, *Renounce the despair.* So I did. *Renounce turning to women and sexual sin.* So I did. *And turning to drugs and alcohol.* I prayed, *Oh Jesus, I do, I renounce it all. I ask your forgiveness. Cleanse me. Come back into those years with me and sanctify my heart.*

Inner healing might be described as sanctifying the past, inviting Jesus back into events and relationships, because for one reason or another he was not invited in at the time. I love that thought—sanctifying the past. Now that we are walking with Jesus, we can invite him into our past and walk with him there too. Much of our hearts were shaped "back then," most of our deep convictions formed. Oh, how I wish I had been a Christian in high school and walked with God during those years. But I wasn't, and so I ask Christ back into those events and relationships as memories surface—or when something like this party stirs longings familiar to those I felt then.

Now I realized that over the past six months or so, God has been taking me back through my high school years. Just today I had a moment that touched something in me and opened a door for more healing. More sanctification. A few weeks ago I bought a diesel pickup. I'm forty-six, but it was the first time I'd ever bought a car because I wanted to, because I liked it, not because the family needed it. A pickup does something for a man that a minivan just can't touch. Anyway, a young gal who works for us was riding along with me to go check on our horses. As she climbed into my truck, she was wowed. She loved it, exclaimed, "I had no idea the interior was like this!" And then, as I fired up the engine, she sighed and said, "I love the sound of a diesel engine."

I felt like The Man.

Now this had nothing to do with the beginnings of an affair. It had everything to do with the past. When I was fifteen, on one of those reckless party-filled Saturday nights, a few buddies and I took my parents' car out joyriding. I got caught, and my folks' reaction was to lay down an edict—I would not get my driver's license until I was eighteen. It wasn't a discipline; it was a punishment. It was over the top. No car, no driving through high school. It was *emasculating*. If I wanted to go see a girl, I had to ride my bike to her house. What a nerd. If I wanted to go on a date, she had to drive. What a little boy, I had to bum a ride to school every day from a friend. What a weenie. I never saw how emasculating this was until today.

Here I'd finally bought a pretty cool truck for myself, with my own cash, and I had this cute girl going nuts over it. It was a new experience. What caught my attention was this thought, or emotion, that leapt up from my heart: *I'm not the idiot.* Wow. How long had that been lying down there? Thirty-two years. Ever since high school.

Hugh Calahan drove this really sweet yellow and black Camaro. It was fast. Danny Wilson had a cool truck with a lift kit, and I remember it did something for him when he bought it. He changed. He walked taller, had a sense of being The Man. He was confident. I never, ever had that. I had no cash, I had no wheels,

I had no strength. If I could have pulled into the parking lot in my diesel truck. If I could have asked a girl on a date and showed up at her house to pick her up. What would that have been like?

Later, in a quiet moment, I am asking Christ into this revelation. *Jesus, come into this. Heal this season of my life, this emasculation. Heal this wound in me.* (How many men make the mistake of thinking, *I just need to nab this cute girl*? It's not the girl. It's the healing we need. She was just the vessel God used to raise the issue.) As I am praying over this and listening to where God is leading, I see myself. I am back in high school. But I'm a Christian. I'm not a stoner anymore. Jesus is with me. I am pulling into the school's parking lot in my diesel truck.

How beautiful is that? Christ can heal our past.

(More at walkingwithgod.net)

A Return to Intimacy

Today is New Year's Day.

Now, I'm not a big New Year's guy myself. Don't ever make resolutions. Don't have much desire to party. I mean, what's the party about? A year passes, a new year begins. I suppose that if you had an amazing year, it might be reason to celebrate, worship God for it. On further reflection I suppose that if you had an awful year, it might be reason to celebrate the fact that it's over. But taken as most people celebrate New Year's Eve, it has always struck me as a pretty hollow attempt to generate a moment of transcendence, a grasp by people who need to feel that something special is taking place because their past year wasn't really all that eventful and maybe, just maybe the coming year will be. Hope springs eternal.

Don't get me wrong—I think milestones are important, and I wish we postmodern Christians had a much richer tradition of holy days, feast days, days of remembrance, and such. Nearly all of that has been lost. Evangelicals for the most part have no concept of holy days, and my experience among Catholics and Episcopalians is that they have long since forgotten the heart of the ceremony they still somewhat observe. (Not everyone, of course. I'm making a general observation.)

Anyhow, as a way of being intentional, our family gave attention to the four weeks of Advent this year. That proved very meaningful, setting aside a month to reflect on Christ's coming to earth and all that it meant and accomplished, and to lift our eyes to the horizon as we look for his return. Christmas deserves a month, not just a day. Advent has a weightiness to it, a deservedness. New Year's feels pretty weak by comparison.

There seems to me to be much better milestones for hoopla and merrymaking. How about the end of the school year and the beginning of summer vacation? Now that's worth a party. Birthdays are worth celebrating. Anniversaries are too. After all, a year of marriage is a feat. The fact that you haven't killed each other is cause for celebration. Back to New Year's—I was thrilled to be able to go to bed at 10:00 this year. Got a good night's sleep (thanks to the prayer), woke up refreshed, and didn't feel as if I'd missed anything at all.

Now, I do have a few friends who take the occasion of the passing of the year to do some reflecting. They'll get out their personal or family calendar and look back, assess. And I do find it worthwhile to stop and ask myself, *What do I want this year to be like? What do I want to change?*—that sort of thing. All that can be very healthy. Staying up until midnight wearing paper hats and drinking too much has long lost its appeal.

But I was asking God this morning what his word for the new year was, if he wanted to say anything about that, set a sort of theme for this year, and much to my surprise, I immediately heard, *Intimacy.* Almost before I finished asking the question. *Intimacy* between God and me. Yes. That sounds really good. Intimacy would be a shift, and a welcome one. A shift away from "Attack the day" and "Get things done" and even the nobler "Endure."

Maybe it's even at the heart of the life I want to live, the source out of which all else flows.

Not Every Gospel Is Equal

I ran into a couple last weekend in the grocery store. I knew them maybe a decade ago; we went to the same church. I was pushing my cart along in the dairy aisle when I heard someone say, "John!" It was one of those embarrassing moments when old acquaintances clearly know me and I vaguely remember them. But for the life of me, I can't recall their names, and so I say, "Hi!" back, with enthusiasm to cover myself. We chatted for a while, but what was so painfully obvious (to me at least) was that we were no longer on the same page. They seemed stuck in a time warp to me—still concerned about the same old issues, still attending the same church, still using the same old language. The pretense we maintained for a few moments was "We're all still in the same old boat, eh?" Just like the good old days.

But we're not and for the rest of the day I was uncomfortable, though I couldn't really explain why. Now I think I have some clarity, but I'm uncomfortable setting it down in black and white for fear of being misunderstood.

Not all gospels are equal.

We've fallen prey to this thinking that it's wrong to draw a distinction between various movements in Christianity or churches or Christians. After all, we know it's wrong to judge. "Do not judge," Jesus said, "or you too will be judged" (Matthew 7:1). This is a good command, by the way. I'm all for it. But the meaning of this warning has gotten twisted into something else altogether. I find that many Christians are uncomfortable, unable even, to make distinctions between various churches and gospels. And they are *really* uncomfortable saying that one is better than another. I recall two different conversations I had with two different friends.

The first was about a Christian college, and the comment I had just made was, "They don't get it." What I was referring to were three issues—that the heart is central to the Christian life, that we are invited into a conversational intimacy with God, and that spiritual warfare is real. Rather core categories. I mean, we weren't talking about the length of Jesus' robe or how many angels can dance on the head of a pin here. What you believe about these issues will profoundly shape the rest of your Christian experience. My friend—who is somewhat loyal to the school—was really upset. "It's not right to say that," she said. "It's arrogant." Now, there is no question that it could be said arrogantly, but I wasn't being arrogant at all. I was making an observation, explaining why I don't want to refer people to this college.

What do you think—is it right or wrong to make observations like that? And voice them?

The second conversation, with a different friend, went along these lines: She was talking about a church we had once both attended, in particular the women's ministry (with which she was familiar), and how the Bible study program they were running was focused on duty and obligation, with a heavy dose of legalism. She said, "That's the last thing women need in their lives, more shame and guilt. They're leading so many women into bondage." She immediately followed this comment with, "I shouldn't have said that. It's wrong to judge. Now God's probably going to come down on me." Her sudden shift caused my heart to sink. For one thing, she was right about the women's ministry, and thus far to my knowledge no one had said it. It *needed* to be said. For another thing, her immediate self-contempt was a classic symptom of the belief I'm describing.

Yes, Jesus told us not to judge. The context is the Sermon on the Mount. He has been teaching his Jewish listeners—a people who had been taught for centuries that righteousness is all about the externals—that there is a higher righteousness that comes from the heart. He says things like, "Don't think you've kept the spirit of the law just because you haven't murdered—do you hate your brother? Don't think you've kept the spirit of the law just because you've never committed adultery—do you want to in your heart?" He is revamping their whole understanding of holiness.

When it comes to judging others, the text reads as follows:

"Do not judge, or you too will be judged. For in the same way you judge others, you will be judged, and with the measure you use, it will be measured to you.

"Why do you look at the speck of sawdust in your brother's eye and pay no attention to the plank in your own eye? How can you say to your brother, 'Let me take the speck out of your eye,' when all the time there is a plank in your own eye? You hypocrite, first take the plank out of your own eye, and then you will see clearly to remove the speck from your brother's eye." (Matthew 7:1–5)

When you live in a system of rules and regulations, it's easy to think you are righteous because you are keeping all the rules. It's pretty tempting to feel better about yourself by comparing your ability to get your act together with somebody else who's not doing so well. "I'm on time to work every day. Jones over there is a royal slacker; he's always late." What you don't know is that Jones has an autistic daughter he has to take across town to child care, and you, my arrogant little poser, live five minutes from work. When it comes to true holiness, Jesus had been saying, "It's the condition of your heart." Now he spoke to the issue of looking at someone else's life. Notice that he didn't say, "Never acknowledge there is a speck in your brother's eye." He said, "Deal with your own life first, and then you will be in a position to help others deal with theirs."

Most Christians know the passage, but they think it means, "Don't ever let yourself get in the mind-set where you think you're right and someone else is wrong." But, how will we know when we *are* right? And how will we help someone who *is* wrong?

Jesus also said, "Stop judging by mere appearances, and make a right judgment" (John 7:24). Wait a second. Now Jesus is telling his followers *to* judge, and carefully. The context of this passage is Jesus' healing of a blind man on the Sabbath and the Jewish leaders being so upset about it that they wanted to kill him. Talk about missing the point. They had come to worship the law, not the God of the law. As with the Sermon on the Mount, Jesus shows them that they missed the *spirit* of the law entirely. "You circumcise a child on the Sabbath. Now if a child can be circumcised on the Sabbath so that the law of Moses may not be broken, why are you angry with me for healing the whole man on the Sabbath? Stop judging by mere appearances, and make a right judgment" (7:22–24).

Jesus says, "You guys just don't get it. I established the Sabbath for your restoration. A day of rest so that you may be restored. Now you're angry with me for restoring a man on the Sabbath?! I want you to start making the right distinctions and not the wrong ones." He does not say, "Don't make any distinctions." He says, "Start making a right judgment."

Let's go to Paul and the Galatian church:

> I am astonished that you are so quickly deserting the one who called you by the grace of Christ and are turning to a different gospel—which is really no gospel at all. Evidently some people are throwing you into confusion and are trying to pervert the gospel of Christ. But even if we or an angel from heaven should preach a gospel other than the one we preached to you, let him be eternally condemned! As we have already said, so now I say again: If anybody is preaching to you a gospel other than what you accepted, let him be eternally condemned! (1:6–9)

Wow. Paul is pretty hacked off here, and pretty vocal about what he sees. Now, you probably know the story—the Galatians had begun to embrace a gospel that said, "Yes, faith in Jesus Christ. We believe in Jesus Christ. *And,* you need to be circumcised, and keep the Law of Moses as well." A different gospel from the one that Jesus and Paul preached. A "sort-of" gospel. Just enough "Jesus" in there to make it sound like the real deal. But it has other ideas and rules in it that are going to take these folks away from the heart of God and the relationship he offers. (There's a good bit of this still going around, by the way.)

It was a matter of profound concern, and Paul wasn't going to ignore it. This letter was (and is) a public document, which would have been read aloud not just in one church, but probably in many. Paul had no problem saying, "Hey, wait a minute! You're wrong about this!" and doing so publicly.

Was Paul "judging"? Well, he was not being arrogant, and he was not exposing the false teachers to justify himself. But he was certainly judging in the sense that Jesus urged—he was making a right distinction between the true and the false, the accurate and the not-so-accurate.

Do you see? Not every gospel is equal. We need to say so.

This idea that both my friends were under—that it is wrong to draw distinctions and make value judgments between various forms of Christianity—this is not helpful. And it's not biblical. But it has a lot of good people trapped in bad churches and programs. There are just enough Jesus words in there to make them sound like Christianity. But they are not preaching the gospel Jesus preached.

Back to the grocery store. This couple I ran into—I think they are really good people. I believe they love God and sincerely want to serve him. It's just that the Christianity they've embraced is a sort of "Christianity *and*." In this case, it's "Christianity *and* conservatism." Now don't get me wrong: my issue is not with conservatism. I'm conservative in most of my values. But the system they are part of seems more concerned about issues of conservative values than it does drawing people into intimacy with God. They don't think the heart is central (in fact, they fear the heart), and they don't make intimacy with God the goal. They don't restore the whole person.

That concerns me.

Not all gospels are equal.

You must draw these distinctions. Don't just stay with the old gang because it's the old gang. Your loyalty is not to a church or a movement, but to Jesus Christ.

A Sanctified Home

I'd love to say we've resolved the sleeping thing. But two nights ago I had a really dark and scary nightmare.

I can't recall it now (and I don't want to try too hard), but it had something to do with an evil house several of us were in, and someone was about to die. It was about 12:30 a.m. when this hit, and it woke me in fear and I began to pray. There was a palpable presence of fear in my room; I certainly felt fear, right there in my sternum. I started bringing the kingdom of God and the authority of Jesus Christ against fear, and every foul spirit in the room. It lifted . . . a little. But I could sense it wasn't gone. I wanted it to be gone; I wanted to go back to sleep. But years of this have taught me to get up and really pray it through. A halfhearted swing at it just doesn't do the trick.

You'd think that the name of Jesus would cause these foul spirits to leave immediately, and sometimes they do. But sometimes they don't (see Mark 9:18). I remember years ago my friend Brent said that dealing with foul spirits is like dealing with IRS agents—they are students of the law, and they know every technical twist and turn of the code. In the case of foul spirits, we've found that quite often you have to name them and bring the work of Christ against them specifically, or they won't leave. Remember— these are fallen, twisted, *disobedient* spirits—their very nature is to defy. Half asleep and half afraid, I was struggling to dial in enough to the Spirit of God to know exactly what I was dealing with and therefore pray effectively. It took some time, maybe fifteen minutes of continual prayer, bringing the work of Christ against fear (I knew at least fear was in the room) "and every dark thing," and sending them to the throne of Jesus Christ. Then I went back to sleep.

The next morning I remembered that I was still awake at midnight when the boys got home from a party, and then it dawned on me that I sensed something come into the house with them. It was a shadow, like when a cloud passes over the sun for a moment. But it was pitch dark in the house when I sensed something darker pass over or through or come in. Why didn't I pray right then? What is it in us that just doesn't want to deal with this stuff? We'd rather roll over, fluff our pillow, and hope it goes away. Well, this one didn't.

Through the course of the day, I felt a lingering haze over my heart and mind. Nothing too obvious, I just wasn't out in the full sunshine of God's loving presence and the life-giving freedom of the Spirit. Late in the afternoon I was downstairs playing pool with the boys, and Blaine was in a bad mood. I teased him about his mood, trying to lift him out of it with humor. A fifty-fifty gamble. I lost. He made a few snarky comments during the game, and I jumped on his case in anger and said, "Change your attitude or get out of the game." (This would be one of those examples of

"Don't do this.") Whatever was dampening Blaine's heart, I had just joined sides with it. He left the room.

At this point I was still not putting two and two together—the nightmare, the recollection that some dark thing passed into our home a half hour before the nightmare, the haze over my heart, and now Blaine's funk. Now I was an unintentional collaborator with whatever this thing was.

Then came dinner, and the boys were firing accusations at each other. "You took the biggest piece of bread." "Stop slurping, you're making me sick." Two of them got up to leave. I was instantly hacked off and ready to come down with a heavy hand (again), but *finally* I woke up to what was going on. "Hey, gang. Something's up here. I think we have a foul spirit present. Let's all pray against this." With a few sighs and a noticeable lack of enthusiasm (which I had to overlook or it would have gotten me more ticked and the prayer would have been a sham), they gathered back around the table and we prayed together. "We bring the work of Jesus Christ and the fullness of his authority against this foul spirit . . ." (In teaching my sons how to pray effective spiritual warfare prayers, I often have them repeat out loud after me.) "And we command this spirit to leave our home in Jesus' name." Okay, that was good.

Then, not thirty seconds later, someone said something snarky and I was jumping in with "You'd better change your attitude." God have mercy. Obviously, our prayers hadn't worked yet.

Blaine had to pick up some homework he left at a buddy's house, so we ran down to get it, and while we were driving along, we were talking about what had been happening. First, I needed to apologize for jumping on his case. You can't win spiritual warfare while you are walking in sin. The foul spirits laugh at that, because you've already jumped in with them. Warfare will make you holy, because you have to be clean to deal with it. I said, "Blaine, I think I hurt your feelings this afternoon."

"Yes, you did."

"I am so sorry, hon."

"I forgive you," he answered.

We drove on for a few more minutes, and then Blaine said, "I'm thinking maybe this warfare came in last night because of the party."

"Yeah, I've been wondering that too. Who all was there?"

It's really important, when you've come under an attack, to assess what the open door might be. Did you watch a creepy movie? Make some agreement during the day? Who were you with last—or who are you about to see? Sometimes it's someone else's warfare. The party was mostly good kids we knew, but there were a couple of troubled boys there. So—not yet knowing fully what we were dealing with or where it came from—we prayed over what we did know. It's sort of like a crime scene—something foul is afoot, and maybe all you have right now is a few fingerprints and no clear suspects—so you start with the process of elimination. I led Blaine in prayer, bringing the cross of Christ against these boys and their warfare, adding, "And I forbid it to transfer to me."

I usually feel awkward and kind of dimwitted whenever I'm trying to teach my sons anything about God, especially spiritual warfare stuff. But a few months ago Blaine was volunteering on the work crew at a retreat when he got hit with discouragement and *Nobody likes you* and *You don't fit here . . . you ought to leave.* He was alone in his bunk, trying to get to sleep, but he couldn't sleep. When the accusations started getting worse, he recognized them as warfare. He later told me, "So I asked myself, 'How would Dad pray about this?' and I remembered what we pray, and it worked. It took two swings, but it left. Like, totally gone."

No matter how awkward you feel, go ahead and pray through this stuff. Out loud. With your family and friends.

Back to the story. We were in the process of elimination, and after praying about the boys he was with, Blaine seemed to be doing better. Then he said, "Hey, wait a minute—what about that dagger Jeremy gave me?"

"What?"

"For my birthday. Jeremy gave me a dagger last night."

Hmm. Sounded suspicious. The detective in me said, *We're onto something now.* When we got home I asked to see the dagger, and it looked "dark"—the design, the black sheath with tooling on it. It looked like something the Orcs might carry in Lord of the Rings.

I asked, "Do you know where Jeremy got this?"

"No."

"Can you ask him?"

"Sure."

In the meantime, we prayed over the knife, cleansing it with the blood of Jesus Christ and binding it under his authority. Because it belonged to Blaine, I had him pray along with me. "And I forbid it to be a channel of any foul thing to me or my home. In Jesus' name."

Conduits. Open doors. The enemy will use anything he can find to assault us or bring trouble into our homes. Start with the obvious. Your Aunt Gladys gives you a beautiful ironwood carving of a Hindu god she picked up on her travels. Do you keep it? "Well, gosh—it was expensive and we don't believe in Hindu gods, so isn't it just a piece of art?" Nope. Hindu gods are demons; this is a statue of a demon. Furthermore, the makers of idols may have chanted a spell (they think it is a "blessing") over those who take the idols into their homes. Bad juju. Get rid of it.

But that's just the obvious. The enemy doesn't want his conduits so easily recognized. We've had popular though dark movies brought into our home, loans from people—even believers— who thought they were great movies. Watch also for books your kids bring home for school assignments. Some video games are tools of the enemy as well. Family "heirlooms" (e.g., something your great-grandfather picked up in a curio shop in Bali) can be associated with spirits. And you may have to clean out albums or CDs you collected before you came to Christ. Heads up! Let this be a category you think about.

Now, I'm not suggesting paranoia. Lots of stuff is benign. But when warfare hits, be a detective. *Is there a conduit? Where did this thing come from? Who did it belong to?* Pray over it; ask God what he thinks. It will prove to be very helpful.

The Bible actually has a lot to say about objects and their holiness or uncleanness. When Josiah conducted his wonderful reforms in Jerusalem and Judah, "the king ordered Hilkiah the high priest, the priests next in rank and the doorkeepers to remove from the temple of the LORD all the articles made for Baal and Asherah and all the starry hosts. He burned them outside Jerusalem in the fields of the Kidron Valley and took the ashes to Bethel" (2 Kings 23:4). *All* the articles, even those related to Baal. There were no doubt the obvious idols. But even common utensils such as tongs used in dark worship were to be removed. The king took conduits seriously.

Now, there is no hard-and-fast law here. You have to follow the Spirit of God and ascertain the spirit of the article in question. Some things can be cleansed and sanctified to God.

When Tou king of Hamath heard that David had defeated the entire army of Hadadezer, he sent his son Joram to King David to greet him and congratulate him on his victory in battle over Hadadezer, who had been at war with Tou. Joram brought with him articles of silver and gold and bronze.

King David dedicated these articles to the LORD, as he had done with the silver and gold from all the nations he had subdued. (2 Samuel 8:9–11)

For example, we don't only listen to "Christian music" in our family. But we are careful to discern what the spirit of the "secular" music is and are sensitive to the fact that certain musicians and bands are just plain dark.

Other things are better simply thrown out, or burned to ash in the Kidron Valley. And you may discover that you can have a conduit in your possession for some time and it doesn't seem to be a channel for evil, but then the enemy comes looking for an open door and finds this object useful to his purposes and it suddenly becomes a problem. The same principle holds true for unconfessed sins in our past or old agreements we have never broken. They may lie dormant for years, but then the enemy finds them or returns to use them for his present schemes. In the same way that we use spiritual attacks to do a personal inventory (*Have I opened the door to this, Lord? Is there something I need to confess, repent of, or break covenant with?*), we find that our households need to be sanctified and kept holy as well.

(More at walkingwithgod.net)

spring
summer
fall
winter

a time of resurrection, recovered hope and desire, a time of new beginnings

Accepting What I Find Hard to Accept

It's snowing outside.

Again.

Geez, flippin' Louise—we are finally into the early days of spring, and twice last week it dumped again, a total of two feet or more. I just got the driveway nice and clear and the roads had finally dried up, and now there's another four or five inches out there. What do I do with this weather?

I grew up in Southern California. We played Frisbee in shorts on Christmas. The plants were green all year round. They have palm trees for heaven's sake. I don't think I even owned a jacket. So this is a big-time adjustment for me. We don't really have a spring in Colorado. Winter holds on with its teeth until May. Then we get a week or two of transition, and suddenly it's summer.

I've always thought of myself as a pretty resilient person (willing to endure), but I am humbled to find how much the weather affects my mood. My attitude. My outlook on life. We have three days of storm and blizzard, and I've got the blues. Then the sun comes out and I'm happy, life is good, and God is near again. Geez. I feel like a groundhog—I'm not coming out unless I see my shadow. Until the sun shines I'm pouting in my hole.

Now, here is the kindness of God. A few weeks ago I am flipping through a magazine and see an article on great places to ski. I am about to blow past it because I don't want to ski. I want summer to come back. I am determined to sulk until it does. Then I ran across this quote in the ad: "To love winter, or to love anything or anybody, you must let go and give yourself over to it."

I knew it was God, because immediately I felt busted. Totally busted, once again. I'm not given over. I'm pouting. I can sense God saying, *Yes, you are. Now stop it.*

Giving myself over to winter would be a really good thing for those who have to live with me, 'cause it isn't any fun to live with a groundhog who's moping around the house constantly griping about the weather (or anything else for that matter). I remember something author Dennis Prager said—that "happiness is a moral obligation." The reason we are morally obligated to be happy is because people have to live with us. If I'm chronically unhappy, or even unhappy for more than a day or two, they pay for it. Would you want to live with Eeyore? Puddleglum? What's it like for the rest of the family when I'm frumping around the house? My unhappiness casts a long shadow. It's not fair to ask them to live under that.

Unhappiness is self-indulgent. It's like insisting that everyone else listen to your taste in music. And it happens to be fugues played on the organ.

Okay. I hear God. I'd better make the best of this weather. Give myself over to it. We have three months of snow to go.

On the Things God Withholds

The weather got me thinking about acceptance and surrender, which then led me to think about more significant, lingering, and long-standing disappointments in my life. I know you have yours too. What are we to make of these things? How do we walk with God in them?

Now, I want to be careful here. There are many reasons for our losses and our unmet desires. The war we live in is reason enough. There *is* a thief, with a whole army behind him, and he and his army steal, kill, and destroy like terrorists. When life isn't good we have to be careful we don't jump to the conclusion *God is withholding this from me.* We jump to it too quickly, as if the only cause-and-effect relationship in this world is God giving or not giving things to us. (Remember A + B = C? That's not how things work.) People can withhold love and kindness, even though God commands them not to. Is it God's fault? And frankly, we sabotage a lot of God's intended joy simply by the way we approach life.

Yet, having said that, there *are* things we are asked to live without. I have my list and you have yours. What am I to do with the fact that despite my walk with God, my willingness to follow, and my resolve to do battle, there are things I have to live without?

As I was praying about my disappointments the other day, I noticed something lingering beneath the surface. I realized that somewhere along the way, I'd come to an agreement of sorts—I *need* this. Not that I want it, and very much. But that *I need it*. It's a very subtle and deadly shift. One that opens the door to despair and a host of other enemies. I was coming to believe that God's love and God's life are not enough. Isn't that what Adam and Eve were seduced into believing—that God was not enough? He had given them so much, but all they could see in their fateful moment of temptation was the one thing they *didn't* have. So they reached for it, even if it meant turning from God.

What was so compelling that Adam and Eve could turn from the living God to reach for the one missing thing? I think I am beginning to understand the answer to that question for myself. We start out longing for something, and the more we come to believe this is what we *have* to have to be happy, the more we obsess about it. The prize just out of reach swells far beyond its actual meaning. It begins to take on mythic proportions. We're certain life will come together once we achieve it. We think, *If only I was married. If only we had children. If only I was rich. If only I had _____* (fill in the blank). Everything else in our lives pales in comparison. Even God. We are falling to believe we *need* whatever is just beyond our reach, and when we fall to this, we are miserable.

I am not minimizing the sorrow of our disappointments. The ache is real. What I am saying is that the ache swells beyond its nature, dominates the landscape of our psyche when we shift from *How I long for this* to *I* need *this*. The only thing we truly need is God and the life he gives us. There is a satisfaction we don't want to come to until we come to it in God. Isn't this the satisfaction warned of in the parable of the rich fool who planned to tear down his barns and build bigger ones?

"The ground of a certain rich man produced a good crop. He thought to himself, 'What shall I do? I have no place to store my crops.'

"Then he said, 'This is what I'll do. I will tear down my barns and build bigger ones, and there I will store all my grain and my goods. And I'll say to myself, "You have plenty of good things laid up for many years. Take life easy; eat, drink and be merry."

"But God said to him, 'You fool! This very night your life will be demanded from you. Then who will get what you have prepared for yourself?'

"This is how it will be with anyone who stores up things for himself but is not rich toward God." (Luke 12:16–21)

The warning is not about cows on the hills and cash in the mattress. The dangerous turn of the soul described here is what happens in the fellow's heart. *I've arrived. Life is good.* But not because he has found his life in God. There is no greater disaster for the human heart than this—to believe we have found life apart from God. And this shift I've been describing—this coming to believe that what I don't have but long for I actually need—is the opening stages of the disaster. For whatever reason, we have come to believe that God is not enough.

And so, whatever else might be the reasons for our disappointments, there is no question that God uses them to draw us to himself. To wean our hearts from every other perceived source of life, so that we might come to find our life in him.

This may be why every one of us bears at least one major and lingering disappointment in our life. God knows what a danger it would be for us to think we've arrived. I'm remembering a scene in *The Legend of Bagger Vance*, where Bagger says to Junuh, "Ain't a soul on this entire earth ain't got a burden to carry that he don't understand." It might be health. Or a relationship. It might be a child, or the fact they have no child. Everyone has a cross to bear. Everyone. It serves to remind us every day that we cannot make life work the way we want. We can't arrive. Not completely. Not yet. If we'll let it, the disappointment can be God's way of continually drawing us back to himself.

I know that I face a choice. I can feel it down inside, and I watch it take place in my heart. I can let my disappointments define my life. Or I can let them take me back to God, to find my life in him in ways I have not yet learned. The rest remains a mystery. But this is enough to know.

And so I break the agreement that I've made, that I need this. I give this place in my heart back to you, God. Fill me with your love and your life, in this very place.

Unmet Longings

There is more to say about the things we have to live without.

What do we then do with these longings and desires that go unmet? I mean, they keep presenting themselves in one way or another.

I think what I do is simply bury them (and I see others do it too). On one hand, of course we do. It feels like we have to. You cannot live your life with a constant awareness of heightened desires that are unmet, just as you can't go through your day continually pining for a life you do not have. You have to live the life you do have. But I find that from time to time God comes and actually stirs our longings and desires, awakens them. You see someone and think, *What would life be like with her (or him)?* Over dinner one night someone tells you how much he loves his job, and you think, *Maybe it's time for a change. I always did want to* _____ (fill in the blank). Be a writer. An architect.

Why does God do this? Wouldn't it be better to let sleeping dogs lie?

No. To bury the deep longings of our hearts is not a good thing. Doing so begins to shut our hearts down, and then we fall into that "get on with life" mentality. For me, that means bearing down and working. Getting things done. But my passion slowly fades away, and life recedes from me. I cannot bring to my work the zest I once did, so even my work suffers. Because my heart is suffering. It's like a form of slow starvation. If your body doesn't get what it needs, you can run for a while without it. But slowly the erosion begins to manifest itself. You get tired, your muscles ache, or you start having headaches or a thousand other symptoms. You need nourishment.

The heart is like that. Thank God, we cannot force it down forever. Hurting, it begins to insist on some attention. Now, we can either listen to those rumblings and let our hearts surface so that we bring them to God, or we can give in to some addiction. The starving heart won't be ignored forever. Some promise of life comes along and *boom*—we find ourselves in the kitchen closet taking down a quart of ice cream or cruising the Internet for some intimacy.

God knows the danger of ignoring our hearts, and so he reawakens desire. You see a photo in a magazine, and pause, and sigh. You see someone with a life that reminds you of the life you once thought you would live. You're channel surfing one night and see someone doing the very thing you always dreamed you would do—the runner breaking the tape, the woman enjoying herself immensely as she teaches her cooking class. Sometimes all it takes is seeing someone enjoying themselves doing anything, and your heart says, *I want that too.*

God does this for our own good. He does it to reawaken desire, to stir our hearts up from the depths we sent them to. He does it so that we don't continue to kill our hearts and so that we don't fall prey to some substitute that looks like life but will become an addiction in short order.

He sometimes does it so that we will seek the life we were meant to seek. Isn't this just what happens to the prodigal? He wakes one day to say, "How many of my father's hired men have food to spare, and here I am starving to death!" (Luke 15:17). "Look at *their* lives," he says. And he is stirred to head for home. To seek life. I have given up on friendship several times in my life—made the subtle agreement to go on without it. But God came and stirred my desire through a scene from a movie, a story a colleague was telling, or an old photograph of a time when I had a good friend. It stirred me to go back and give friendship another try. Don't give up.

I know God does this in marriage. A woman we know abandoned hope for intimacy with her husband years ago. *It could be worse*, she said to herself. And years went by. Then something awakened her desire—a romance she saw in a movie or the intimacy she witnessed in the marriage of some friends. The longing may have seemed like an unwelcome intruder. Maybe it would only cause more pain. Or maybe she would do something stupid. But it became the force by which she sought counseling, and invited her husband to join her. It opened a door toward life.

More often than not this awakening of desire is an invitation from God to seek what we've given up as lost, an invitation to try again. This has been true in my marriage as well. It's so easy to just reach those plateaus where we decide, *This is good enough. It could be better, but it could be worse too. To get to the better will take work, and risk, and I'm fine with things the way they are.* God comes along and says, *Don't give up.*

I'm stunned by this whole reawakening process. The willingness and what feels like such a risk for God to reawaken desire in me. I mean, geez—to feel again a desire I've long buried. Yikes. I might make a wrong move, come to the wrong conclusion, just as our friend might have decided that what she really needed was a different spouse.

Something I read years ago by C. S. Lewis in *The Weight of Glory* has proven helpful to me time and time again, and may rescue us in the very moment of awakened desire I am describing. Lewis is trying to show us that what God uses to awaken desire is *not* necessarily what we long for. The things "in which we thought the beauty was located will betray us if we trust to them; it was not *in* them, it only came *through* them, and what came through them was longing. These things . . . are good images of what we desire; but if they are mistaken for the thing itself, they turn into dumb idols, breaking the hearts of their worshippers. For they are not the thing itself." They are not what we are longing for.

It is not that specific man or woman we desire, but what they point to, what is coming through them. They are a picture of what we long for. Like the girl in my diesel truck. It wasn't about her. God used her to awaken a longing, to get to a long-buried part of my heart so that he could heal me. When a desire is awakened, by whatever source, the thing to pray is, *God, what do you have for me?*

I think many of us who do long for a holy life have chosen the way of "kill desire," because at the time it seems there is no other way. And sometimes, in the moment, this may well be our only choice. Certainly it is better to push away some longing if we know that yielding to it means giving way to temptation. But this is not the best way to holiness in the long run, for the starving heart will eventually seek some relief.

But there are desires that we know cannot be met now.

It may be too late to become a professional baseball player or musician, too late to have a child. This is the real danger zone, because it seems like there is no other choice but to put away this part of your heart. But to send your heart into exile because your longings have no hope of being met is also to exile your heart from the love of God. And he would have your whole heart. It's hard to tell whether God is arousing some desire so that you may seek a new life or simply so that this part of your heart may be made whole in him. But whatever else may be the case, you have to begin by giving this part of your heart back to God. Above all else, *your heart must find a safe home in him.*

(More at walkingwithgod.net)

Resting

I am so grateful I listened to God last week.

Tomorrow, Wednesday, I fly to San Diego to speak at a conference—two sessions, one in the afternoon and one in the evening. Get to bed late, then jump on an early morning flight on Thursday back to Colorado, just in time to head into our four-day Wild at

Heart retreat we're doing here. I don't normally stack missions back to back like this. I've learned the hard way that it's not a good thing to do. But it happened. Last week I saw these demands coming like a huge wave, swelling bigger and bigger as it approaches the shore. So I prayed, *Lord, what do I need to be prepared for next week?* He told me to take Monday and Tuesday off. What gracious counsel. I wouldn't have done it otherwise. I would have jumped into the normal routine, tried to get as much off my desk as I could before I left, and headed into these events exhausted.

But I didn't blast out the door and charge into the day, thinking about all that needs to get done. Instead, I had a leisurely breakfast. Read a magazine. Took time to pray. It's warm today, a really wonderful break from all the snow we've been having, and I've been enjoying working outside, chipping away the ice from my driveway with a pickax. It's not work, not to me. It's fun. And rest. The rest is so good.

I know I've disrupted a few people who did not take time for their hearts, challenged their decision to take on the week just as I would have, had I not asked God. I don't know if they asked for advance words or not or heeded what they heard. But it's disrupting to walk with God. And inviting too.

Sorting Things Out

What do I do with this? I've just left the table where the boys and I were having dinner tonight. (Mom is at a women's Bible study.) I heard that the weather was supposed to be good this weekend, and I asked the boys rather hopefully (and feeling like a good and generous dad), "Who'd like to go bird hunting this weekend?" In my heart I wanted a joyful and grateful response. "Wow! I do!" "No, no, take me!" Instead, there was silence. A long silence, as each of them sat awkwardly wondering, *How do I say I don't want to go?* One by one they said something to the effect of "Not really." I felt so dismissed.

It was all I could do not to sulk.

I know my boys are teenagers now. I know they are developing lives of their own. But still I was hurt. Disappointed. And something like lonely. Still am, as I come into my office to try and sort this out. I need to sort this out. (Don't just let your internal world roll on unrecognized and unshepherded.) Part of me wanted to let them know I was hurt (and defensive) right away. "Fine. I'll ask one of the guys. I know *they* want to go." *You little twerps. Think of all the young men out there who are dying for someone to take them anywhere. You ingrates just don't know what you are turning down.*

Okay. I know I'm hurt, and I'm wondering if what's really hurting me is losing my boys to growing up. Moms hit this moment, too, when their boys head off to college or simply reach that stage they only want to do "guy stuff" with Dad. To be honest, I miss that stage. There was a time when doing anything with Dad was a really big treat. "I'm going down to wash the car—anybody want to come?" "I do!" they'd yell in unison and race for the door. A trip to Home Depot was an adventure. A weekend camping might well have been a safari to Mozambique.

But not anymore.

I know—I hope—the day will come when they will realize what I have offered as a father. When a day spent with me sounds really good again. I think this is also part of growing up. You first hit that stage in your teens when your friends are far more interesting than your dad. Then you head off to college, and there are all sorts of things going on that seem a lot more exciting than bird hunting with the old man. Girls will take their attention away too. Then it's work. (I'm suddenly hearing the lines to "Cat's in the Cradle"—"What I'd really like, Dad, is to borrow the car keys. See you later. Can I have them please?" and I am ready to weep.)

But there comes another day when you begin to feel the need and the hunger for the presence of your father. For some guys it comes as they get out of college and face real life and realize they need some counsel and help. Or it might be a few years into marriage or at the birth of a child. Or maybe several years into work. The buddies are all moved away, the parties are over, and now you begin to realize you need a source of wisdom and strength and love that's been there all along but you've never really appreciated it. This was my journey and the journey of many men I counsel. Except, for most of us, Dad is no longer here to offer help. Then you *really* know what you missed.

When will my boys realize this? I don't know. I only pray they do. And what will I do in the meantime? If I don't sort this out, I'll carry a resentment toward them, if only subtly. But they'll sense it, and it will hurt our relationship. I won't want to invite them next time. A gap will grow there. They'll see that Dad is acting way immature, and they won't want to talk about something else like this when it comes up. That awkwardness that creeps in between parents and their children—this is how it starts. All because we won't sort out our internal issues for ourselves. This stuff festers down inside if we let it roll on unchallenged, unconsidered.

Now the evening is wearing on. I am trying—with God's help—to shepherd my heart through this. Soon I will say good night to my boys. In what mood?

What is it that I need in this moment, God? I do know this—I know I need you to come and minister to me here. Jesus, come and meet me here, in this disappointment and hurt that I am feeling. I wanted my boys to be excited. I want them to see time with me as a highlight. It hurts to have my sons grow up and begin to pull away. It hurts to be dismissed for stuff like Xbox and movies and girlfriends. Meet me here.

I also know this: I know I don't want to punish them for not choosing me. Jesus, help me to love them even when they turn me down. Help me to love them and value them even when they take up hobbies and interests quite different from mine. Help me to love them as they pull away.

And now, at the end of all this journaling, my thoughts turn to you as my Father. I am embarrassed and pained to think how true all that I've just penned could be said of me toward you. That is, how much have you offered of yourself and I've chosen other things? I'm silenced. Stopped. All I can say is forgive me. You are more gracious and long-suffering than I can ever say. I want to be a better son.

As I said at the start of this book, life will present us with hundreds of opportunities in a single week to take a look at our internal world, to walk with God there, to become more fully his. Don't let your internal life go unshepherded.

(More at walkingwithgod.net)

Assault

The past four days have been brutal. An emotional mugging. Jungle warfare—a dark and hazy firefight with seduction, condemnation, pride, diminishment, and Lord knows what else. I got ambushed, and my heart is still struggling to recover.

I had traveled back East for a conference. Some important relationships were at risk, as well as the future of the message I am trying to bring. I felt prepared, but I think I underestimated all that was at stake. At least, that's what I'm thinking now, because the enemy really came on with a vengeance.

The first few sessions of the conference go well. I feel like I am acting with integrity. Then something shifts. What I notice is a suggestion of seduction and lust toward a woman involved. I reject it and press on. A few minutes later it returns, this time with a dose of pride. Again I reject it. I am trying to stay focused on the event, stay true, honor my colleagues, walk with God. But this stuff is coming on strong.

It felt as though the enemy was probing the perimeter, looking for a weakness. Lust. Then arrogance. Now distraction. Again and again. I think the conference gave me enough to concentrate on to maintain focus, sort of like driving in a rainstorm. You bear down, double your concentration, grip the wheel. But after my redoubled efforts I felt like crap. After holding off what the enemy had thrown at me, I felt like he then sent the big boys.

A deep distress now enters in. Judgment galore. None of this is taking a verbal form, but the overwhelming sense is, *Look at you. You call yourself a man of God. You are utterly corrupt inside. And God is now far away.*

There's a scene from *Pilgrim's Progress* that would help us all to keep in mind.

One thing I would not let slip; I took notice that now poor Christian was so confounded that he did not know his own voice; and thus I perceived it. Just when he was come over against the mouth of the burning pit, one of the wicked ones got behind him, and stepped up softly to him, and whisperingly suggested many grievous blasphemies to him, which he verily thought had proceeded from his own mind. This put Christian more to it than any thing that he had met with before, even to think that he should now blaspheme him that he loved so much before; yet if he could have helped it, he would not have done it; but he had not the discretion either to stop his ears, or to know from whence these blasphemies came.

Christian could not discern his own voice. He doesn't know where these blasphemies came from. He believed they were coming from his own heart, and he was devastated. That's exactly how I felt. Devastated. How could I do this to my Lord? I was in anguish thinking that this was the true condition of my heart. Now devastated, the enemy pours on contempt and judgment and the ongoing sense that God had withdrawn.

Sorting out what is really going on is hard at these times. What is genuine conviction, and what is assault? What is my fault, and what is warfare? And where is the warfare coming from? Start with this: you shall know them by their fruit. Genuine conviction brings repentance—not judgment or contempt. Genuine conviction brings us back to God. It doesn't say to us, *You've blown it so badly he has removed himself from you.* I had to start with the fruit of my situation—I was deeply distressed. I felt anguish. And I felt far from God. These things were not from the Holy Spirit. At the time, that's about all I knew.

So I begin to bring the work of Christ against the assault. But, man, is it hard. I am having to pray every thirty minutes or so. Something has a foothold here.

To fight effectively I have to take responsibility for what part *is* mine. I opened the door to pride. I entertained it. I now see that the enemy was trying to penetrate my defenses by breaking down my integrity any way he could. He found an agreement with pride. It came in when I saw how well things were going and the influence I was having, and I let my heart go to, *You are really something.* So I confess and renounce the pride, the arrogance. I give God the glory for all that happened.

Pride was just the open door the enemy gained. I turned there for a moment and entertained it. Then *boom*—in came the enemy's real goal—deep distress and the contempt and judgment that go with it.

But wait a minute—if my heart is evil, then why does it distress me so deeply to think so? If I really do want lust, seduction, arrogance, and all that stuff, why am I grieved to think that I do?

That makes no sense. If I actually *want* to walk away from God, why does it bring *anguish* to entertain the thought of doing so? This is not my true heart. This is not my true desire. I have to fight this distress, contempt, and judgment. This is where the battle is raging. If I give in to this, I will lose intimacy with God. And I will lose heart and all that goes with losing heart. But I am utterly helpless against this distress so long as I think I deserve it, so long as I mistake it for conviction.

I am deep in the jungle of the assault, and the only verse I can even remember to hang on to is, "Count yourselves dead to sin but alive to God in Christ Jesus" (Romans 6:11). I repeat it to myself. Over and over. It gives me strength to fight the distress, contempt, and judgment.

It's day four. The enemy seems to be weakening.

I have to remember this: the issue is never the presenting sin.

The issue is the surrender, however subtle, of our hearts. The open door, the agreement. What follows is the enemy's real goal—our separation from God and from our true selves. I think most Christians never see the battle. They think they crave evil things, and they embrace the resulting contempt for their own hearts as true conviction. Then they assume that, of course, God is going to be distant and they live under all of that for years. "My heart is evil. I am such a wretch. Of course God is distant." They think that's the Christian life.

But it's not.

Or at least, it doesn't have to be. Remember Christian in the valley of the burning pits. Remember where this stuff really comes from. This isn't your true heart—this is your enemy. Fight back. Guard your heart. The assault will lift, if you hold fast.

Lent

It has been a few years—fourteen, now that I think about it—since we were in a church that celebrated Lent. We attended an Episcopal church in town back then and enjoyed it very much. It was there that we learned something of the observance of Lent, that forty-day period of personal preparation leading to the celebration of Easter. A time when many people choose to go without something, such as coffee or CNN, just as Christ fasted for forty days in the wilderness. When this is approached in the spirit of making extra room for God in your life—as opposed to just cutting out caffeine or television—it can be very meaningful.

As I said, it has been some time since Lent was on my radar, and it caught me a little off guard when in our staff meeting yesterday Morgan said, "Why don't we ask Christ what he'd have us give up for Lent. And what he would have us take up." So we did. In a few quiet moments, we asked, *Lord, what would you have me give up for Lent this year?* Now, in my previous days of Lenten observance, alcohol was a leading contender for that thing I-don't-want-to-give-up-and-therefore-probably-should. But I knew drinking wasn't going to be an issue—that's been gone for a while now. As I tried to quiet the clamor inside and sat with the question, repeating to Christ slowly, several times over, *What would you have me give up?* this is what I heard:

Self.

Self? I asked, to make sure I'd heard right.

Self.

Self seems like a biblical thing to surrender, but it isn't quite clear to me what God means by the word. I start trying to fill in the blanks, make some sense of it. Self-obsession? Self-centered-ness? No more clarity on that one, and the gang was moving on to question number two: *And what would you have me take up?*

My love.

Wow. Give up self. Take up his love. It's not what I expected. And it had all the danger of striking at something deep in me. That sounded like God. I flagged it in my mind as something to give more time to later and went on with the day. I got back to it this morning. Sometimes when I'm trying to bring myself into focused attention on God and what he is saying, I journal. I write down my thoughts and questions, and as I do I listen for God's response and guidance. Then I write that down as well.

What is the self thing I am to give up, Lord? Obsession. Okay, it's self-obsession. I know what this means—that hyper self-awareness thing I do. Giving it up sounds wonderful. And next to impossible.

I continue to write and listen. *Yes, Jesus. I adore you. Yes. How do I give up self-obsession? By looking to my love in you.* Wow. That makes so much sense to me. This is so right on with all that God has been saying and doing to try to get me to shift over to his love. *I do, I do, I do want to return to your love in me. Say more, Lord— how do I get there? What's that look like? What do I look to now?*

Pause. When God begins to shine his light on some issue in my life, be it internal or some issue taking place around me, I often have a hunch where things might be leading. You know what I mean—I see Christians do this all the time. We get a glimpse of what God might be up to, and we start speculating and filling in the blanks, bringing all our biases and inclinations to it instead of simply listening to him for more. For example, you sense God prompting you to help your parents financially, and you're already inclined to do that, so you just go and do it without stopping to ask, *Now? How much?* Or, you sense God's conviction on a long-standing sin in your life. Being inclined to self-contempt and beating yourself up, you just jump to, *I knew it. It's my fault. I'm the idiot,* and you start making all your plans and resolutions to change (despite the fact that it never works). If you'd stayed with God on the matter, you might have heard his love and tenderness and his gentle counsel for a different way of handling it.

Filling in the blanks. That's what this is. We are constantly filling in the blanks of what we *think* God is up to instead of asking him. It isn't helpful. It's taking the ball and running with it, leaving God behind. Ask the next question, remember?

So I am lingering, quieting my own hunches about where this is headed, neither ignoring them nor letting them write the rest of the script. *Say more, Lord—how do I get there? What's that look like? What do I look to now?* What I meant by "look to now" is, if I am not looking to his love in me, where *am* I looking? I have a pretty good idea, but I want to hear his thoughts on it.

Your ability to stay on top of things.

Right. Busted. Caught with my hand in the cookie jar. I love it when God does that. It is a wonderful sort of nakedness, to have him name the very thing we are doing and trying to hide, or doing and not even knowing it because we've been doing it for so long it has become normal. This sort of conviction has no shame to it. I knew that what he named is exactly what I do. I place all my confidence in my ability to "get it done," "get it right," "stay on top of things." No wonder I feel like I'm "just barely" walking with God. *Forgive me,* I write, *It's so utterly unfaithful, so godless and self-reliant.*

Now, to add to the beauty of the story, for the past couple mornings when I've sat down at the table to have a quick bowl of oatmeal, I've opened my Bible to read a bit, and both times it just opened to Psalm 41. Here is what I read: "I said, 'O LORD, have mercy on me, / heal me, for I have sinned against you'" (41:4).

Do you hear David's approach to God? He doesn't expect to get slammed. He doesn't just promise to repent and do better. He knows he has turned from God, and he knows what he needs is healing. So this is what I prayed: *I ask you to heal the things in me that have led to this self-obsession, this looking to my ability to get it done, get it right, stay on top of things. Forgive me. I want to be centered in your love in me. You in me. Heal me.*

Seeking Guidance

I'm trying to figure out whether or not we should go to Moab this year. And right now, it's not really clear.

For the past seven years a group of guys have made a sort of pilgrimage to the deserts of Moab, Utah. We go in late April or early May, about that time we cannot bear the cold of Colorado for one more weekend. It's warm in Moab by then—usually in the eighties, and we spend four or five days rock climbing, mountain biking, and goofing around. A classic guys' trip. Camping. No showers. Playing Frisbee. Swimming naked. Great campfire stories. It's a trip that has become an icon of our fellowship as men. A highlight of our year for sure.

But this year's trip isn't looking good. Several of the guys who usually come can't make it. There's only one weekend available in the calendar, and it's earlier than we like to go. We are, all of us, really, really busy. It looks like Moab is just going to be tanked. By default.

I'm praying about it, trying to get some guidance. My first question is, *Do we fight for the trip, Lord—or just let it go this year?* It would be so easy to let it go. It makes sense to let it go. As I said, life is really busy right now for all of us. And when life feels busy, isn't our knee-jerk response to say no to stuff like this? I can't take a few days off right now. I have too much to do. Even though we love the Moab trip. Even though it's precious to us. Even though it's the very thing we need to rescue us from the busyness. Remember—we need joy. Lots and lots of joy.

Pause. Isn't this our first reaction, when life seems overwhelming—we start lightening the load, dumping cargo overboard so we don't drown? The problem is, we can dump the wrong things overboard! We think nothing of tossing over joy while hanging on to the very things that overwhelm us.

So I'm seeking God on this. Only the clarity isn't coming right away.

When we are seeking God for clarity and it's not coming, what we need to do first is pay attention to our own posture. What are we feeling? What are our desires? It's a given that where we are will affect our ability to hear God or color what we do hear. I'm torn about this year's trip. On the one hand, I really want to go. I love Moab, love the first warmth of summer, the first real green, the beauty of the desert, the adventures, the time with men. We have never regretted going, not even two years ago when it rained. On the other hand, it's a hassle. I'm busy. I have this book to finish. Nobody else seems to be fighting for it. It would be far easier to let it go.

How many precious things do we let go, give up, surrender because it seems that life is too busy, it's a hassle to fight through to make it happen, or we assume we know what's best or inevitable, and we don't even stop to ask God? We need to stop and ask—*especially* when it seems like giving up some joy is inevitable. God might not agree.

You see, the pace of life in this world creates a momentum to our lives. Like cars on a freeway. And the truth is, quite often God's desire for us will run against that prevailing current. *Get off at the next exit.* His guidance sometimes (often?) seems counter-intuitive. It would be easier to let Moab go this year. Race on by. Everybody's busy. And it won't be the same without the whole group of guys who have made the trip what it was in the past. On the other hand, Sam and Jesse may be headed off to college in the fall, and it's not likely they'll be able to make it for next year's trip. This could be the end of an era. The last of its kind. And how will we *really* feel about letting it go when it's late April and there's two feet of snow outside and we're going stir-crazy?

Even now, I'm trying to see into the future to figure out

what's best. I'm filling in the blanks. We all do that. We try to figure it out. It's not the same thing as walking with God. We simply don't see all that God sees. God says, "My thoughts are not your thoughts" (Isaiah 55:8). He knows what's ahead. He knows what we need. So ask him. I am asking, but the reception isn't superclear right now. I don't have a signal. So what I've done is write out the questions on a pad of paper, one at a time:

"Do we fight for Moab this year? Or let it go?"

This way I can sit with the question before God, praying, listening specifically on one issue at a time without all the other evidence pro and con clouding my thoughts. One question at a time, without weighing all the facts back and forth in my mind. I am not trying to figure it out. I'm trying to hear from God. There is a difference. "My thoughts are not your thoughts," remember?

Sometimes I'll let the pad of paper sit on my desk for a week and pray over it from time to time before I'm confident that I've heard from God. But today, after a few moments, I hear him saying, *Fight for it.* (Actually, that's what I heard him say a few days ago while praying about it as I drove to work. But it seemed so counterintuitive, I didn't trust it. Or maybe at the time it just seemed like a hassle and I didn't *want* to hear it.) Fight for it? Really? *Really.* Okay. Fight for it.

Notice your reaction as you begin to close in on what you believe God is saying. If it produces joy, you're onto something. If it produces sorrow (or fear, or discouragement), stop and ask why. Don't leave your heart behind in this process. I notice my reaction is good, and hope for the trip begins to rise in my heart. (I'd written it off.) I realize that though it would be easier to let it go, my true desire is to make the trip happen. I don't know that

I would have gotten back to my true desire had I not prayed about this. It was buried under all sorts of stuff.

I have my first piece of guidance. We are supposed to fight for this joy. (And you will have to fight for joy, friends. Remember that.) But the puzzle isn't solved yet. The conversation doesn't end here. *When* we go is a big issue as well. I have to ask about that, too, or I could charge ahead and be just as mistaken as not having asked about going on the trip at all. Don't just stop with the first question. Ask the next question.

Late April is a gamble with the weather. It has been chilly a few times when we've gone in April, but it has always been warm when we've gone in May. We want warm. May makes sense. But I don't see how we could possibly pull it off in May. (There I go again, trying to figure it out.) So I write on the page:

"April?"

"May?"

I hear *April 21–24*, which is the weekend we do have open for this. Okay. We're going to Moab, and we're going in April. Something in me feels a little "out there" with where this is landing. I realize I'm going to need to trust God on this. Smile. Isn't that the point—that we trust God enough to follow him? That we live by faith? The Christian life is not the commonsense life. Oswald Chambers said that the only explanation for a Christian's life has to be the existence of God. Otherwise, it makes no sense. I'm really comforted by that. My life often feels like it makes no sense.

Now, I'm not encouraging a senseless approach to life. I'm not saying that you should follow every thought that passes through your head. There is wisdom, and there is revelation. They go together, hand in hand. "I keep asking that the God of our Lord Jesus Christ, the glorious Father, may give you the Spirit of wisdom and revelation, so that you may know him better" (Ephesians 1:17). From the Spirit come both wisdom and revelation. We need them both to walk with God, need them in generous doses to navigate the dangerous waters of this world. If you're the sort of person who tends to lean toward revelation (just asking God for direct guidance), then you need to balance your approach with wisdom. If you lean toward a wisdom approach to life, you must deliberately and consciously include revelation. Ask God.

And if you operate for the most part with neither, you are in real trouble.

Knowing that, we need to admit that risk is always involved when we encourage others to walk with God. People have done a lot of really stupid things in the name of following Jesus. For that reason there are folks in the church who don't want to encourage this sort of risk, this "walking with God." Over the centuries they have tried to eliminate the messiness of personal relationship with Jesus by instituting rules, programs, formulas, methods, and procedures. Those things may have eliminated some of the goofy things that happen when people are encouraged to follow God for themselves. But they also eliminated the very intimacy God calls us to.

What's Jesus' take on the issue?

> "When you are brought before synagogues, rulers and authorities, do not worry about how you will defend yourselves or what you will say, for the Holy Spirit will teach you at that time what you should say." (Luke 12:11–12)

> "It is written in the Prophets: 'They will all be taught by God.' Everyone who listens to the Father and learns from him comes to me." (John 6:45)

"The man who enters by the gate is the shepherd of his sheep. The watchman opens the gate for him, and the sheep listen to his voice. He calls his own sheep by name and leads them out. When he has brought out all his own, he goes on ahead of them, and his sheep follow him because they know his voice." (John 10:2–4)

"But the Counselor, the Holy Spirit, whom the Father will send in my name, will teach you all things and will remind you of everything I have said to you." (John 14:26)

"Here I am! I stand at the door and knock. If anyone hears my voice and opens the door, I will come in and eat with him, and he with me." (Revelation 3:20)

Don't surrender this treasure of intimacy with God just because it can get messy. Walk with God—wisdom *and* revelation—all the while seeking the holiness we know he is after.

The next thing on my pad is "Who?" Who goes is an issue. I think I want to go back to the guys who said, "It just doesn't work for me this year," and ask them to pray about it. Make sure they've asked God about it. I'm going to fight for joy.

(More at walkingwithgod.net)

New Beginnings

Over dinner last night Stasi announces, "I think it's time we get a puppy."

It is an awkward moment and a really vulnerable move on her part. The boys are silent. Caught off guard. My first reaction is *That's all I need. You let yourself love something, and you're just going to lose it in the end. I don't want to go through that again.* Thankfully, I don't say this out loud. She looks to me for some sign of a positive response. I nod and she tells us about what's been surfacing in her heart and the research she's been doing on the Internet. Then the whopper—she shows us some pictures of puppies. I'm convinced God gave the world puppies to soften our hearts. As we look at photos of some Newfoundland and Bernese mountain puppies, my heart begins to drop its guard. If a puppy can't soften your heart, I don't know what will.

Jesus? I ask in my heart. It is just a simple question, meaning, *What do you think about this? What do you want to say? What are your thoughts on the matter?*

Slowly but surely I've been choosing this as my first response to any issue. If I don't intentionally and quickly ask Jesus what he thinks, I'm stunned by how fast my heart can react to a conversation or event. In a nanosecond I can jump to conclusions, make agreements, dismiss people. We all do this. Then we just move on. But we can be dead wrong. We might be in a bad mood. We're certainly biased. And who knows what else is influencing us on any given day?

Jesus?

I find myself doing that a lot these days. It allows him to speak into the moment as life is happening. It gives God a chance to be part of the process rather than my looking to him later, after the damage has been done.

Jesus?

It would be good.

The litters Stasi found are going to be available in a couple of months. I'm watching my internal posture. Will I accept this? Will I be open to it? Will I allow my heart to be open? This is about more than just a puppy. It's about my yieldedness to God, and it's about hope. I don't want to live a defensive life, constantly steeling myself against the future, wary to trust, wary to believe. I want to be open to all God has for me. I want to live the life he wants me to live. All of that's playing out right here, looking at pictures of puppies. This is where it all gets lived out. In the moment.

I believe Christianity is at its core a gospel of life. I believe great breakthrough and healing are available. I believe we can prevent the thief from ransacking our lives if we will do as our Shepherd says. And when we can't seem to find the healing or the breakthrough, when the thief does manage to pillage, I believe ours is a gospel of resurrection. Whatever loss may come, that is not the end of the story. Jesus came that we might have life.

It sounds like a puppy is in our future.

Returning to Love

This morning my thoughts came back to "My love."

I bought a new journal this week because my old one had filled up, and I had more time this morning than usual to linger with God before heading into the day. So I pour myself a cup of coffee, sit down on the couch, and pull out the journal. I always feel strange about writing on the first page of a new journal—all those clean, white pages, nothing yet having been set down. It feels momentous. Kind of like a new beginning. Or at least a new era. What will unfold? And what should I put on the first page? I always have this feeling that it needs to be significant. After all, this is the opening page of a new book in my life, the next chapter with God. It seems to deserve something weighty. Something transcendent.

Looking down at the blank page, I quietly ask God in my heart, *What needs to go here?*

You know what he said.

My love.

So that is what I write down. That is all I write on that opening page. Two words. "My love." It is more than enough. Whatever else gets written in this journal, whatever stories told, whatever prayers, all the processing of life, let it all come under this. Let it be a continuation of this. His love. I sit there and look at it—let it sink in. I am turning my heart toward his love. Letting it be true. Letting it be life to me.

What else, Lord?

Believe my love.

Yes, I do. I believe your love.

And something in me is shifting. I am coming to believe it more than I ever have. It is changing me. I feel less driven. Less compulsive. Less grasping. And less empty. I feel like I want to stay here. To live in his love.

In Closing

As I explained in the introduction, what I have attempted in these pages was to faithfully record what a year's experience of walking with God looks like. Feels like. Sounds like. As I read back over my words, they seem true to what has happened. And yet, so very incomplete. There are *hundreds* more stories I could have told, had I room to tell them. A lot goes on in a year of our lives, doesn't it? I don't want to leave a wrong impression—these stories are a sampling, offered in hopes of shedding light on your own story, helping you learn to hear the voice of God and walk with him whatever may come your way. I hope they have at least been alluring—this sort of relationship with God *is* available. To us all. My greater hope is that these stories have been instructive, and you are finding this walk yourself.

But there is so much more I want to say.

Some of that is contained in my other books, listed at the end of this book. You might also want to drop by walkingwithgod.net, where you'll find dozens of resources to help you in your walk with God. May I also strongly suggest reading through this book again—I know I'm always amazed how much more I get out of a book on a second reading. There is also a workbook that goes along with this book—*A Personal Guide to Walking with God.* What a wonderful idea it would be, to take your time and dive even more deeply into these themes, maybe do so with a few friends. For as I also said in the introduction, learning to walk with God is our deepest need. Everything else in your life depends on it. Don't let anything hold you back from this great treasure.

Several months have passed since I turned in this manuscript. Many more stories have unfolded. We went to Moab, and it was wonderful. Just what we needed, just as God said. My sleep has been good and then not so good. There has been a great deal more healing of my past. I saw a hawk last week, and a golden eagle. I got back on a horse. I lost an old friend in an automobile accident. God has been guiding my reading of Scripture, and it has been very rich. I have also had to break a number of new agreements I made with the enemy. In other words, life has continued to unfold as it does for all of us, with this one important difference—walking with God. I don't know how I ever lived without it (and there were many years I lived without it). This conversational intimacy has become an essential part of my every day. I cannot even begin to say how thankful I am for it.

Oh, and we have a new puppy in the house. His name is Oban. He's a golden retriever. And he won't give me the ball.

(More at walkingwithgod.net)

Acknowledgments

My deepest thanks to the people whose stories are interwoven with mine in these pages—my family, my friends, my allies at Ransomed Heart, at Thomas Nelson, and Yates and Yates.

Appendix: The Daily Prayer

Over the years I have grown in my understanding of prayer and spiritual warfare and of our need to be restored in the life of God each day. And so I have developed this prayer, which I call "The Daily Prayer." I call it that because I pray it daily. Before anything else. Even breakfast. The prayer has morphed through several versions as I've learned something new about the work of Christ for us or the ploys of the enemy. And so I offer you this, the latest version. May it be a source of life to you. Daily.

MY DEAR LORD JESUS, I come to you now to be restored in you, to be renewed in you, to receive your love and your life and all the grace and mercy I so desperately need this day. I honor you as my Sovereign, and I surrender every aspect of my life totally and completely to you. I give you my spirit, soul, and body, my heart, mind, and will. I cover myself with your blood—my spirit, soul, and body, my heart, mind, and will. I ask your Holy Spirit to restore me in you, renew me in you, and to lead me in this time of prayer. In all that I now pray, I stand in total agreement with your Spirit and with my intercessors and allies, by your Spirit alone.

[Now, if you are a husband, you'll want to include your wife in this time of prayer. If you are a parent, you'll want to include your children. If this doesn't apply to you, jump to the paragraph following this one.]

In all that I now pray, I include (wife and/or children, by name). Acting as their head, I bring them under your authority and covering, as I come under your authority and covering. I cover (wife and/or children, by name) with your blood—their spirits, souls, and bodies, their hearts, minds, and wills. I ask your Spirit to restore them in you, renew them in you, and apply to them all that I now pray on their behalf, acting as their head.

Dear God, holy and victorious Trinity, you alone are worthy of all my worship, my heart's devotion, my praise, all my trust, and all the glory of my life. I love you, I worship you, I trust you. I give myself over to you in my heart's search for life. You alone are life, and you have become my life. I renounce all other gods and all idols, and I give you the place in my heart and in my life that you truly deserve. I confess here and now that this is all about you, God, and not about me. You are the hero of this story, and I belong to you. Forgive me for my every sin. Search me and know me and reveal to me where you are working in my life. Grant to me the grace of your healing and deliverance and a deep and true repentance.

Heavenly Father, thank you for loving me and choosing me before you made the world. You are my true Father—my Creator, my Redeemer, my Sustainer, and the true end of all things, including my life. I love you, I trust you, and I worship you. I give myself over to you to be one with you in all things, as Jesus is one with you. Thank you for proving your love by sending Jesus. I receive him and all his life and all his work, which you ordained for me. Thank you for including me in Christ, for forgiving me my sins, for granting me his righteousness, for making me complete in him. Thank you for making me alive with Christ, raising me with him, seating me with him at your right hand, establishing me in his authority, and anointing me with your Holy Spirit, your love, and your favor. I receive it all with thanks and give it total claim to my life—my spirit, soul, and body, my heart, mind, and will. I bring the life and the work of Jesus over my life today [wife and/or children, by name] and over my home, my household, my vehicles, my finances—all my kingdom and domain.

Jesus, thank you for coming to ransom me with your own life. I love you, I worship you, I trust you. I give myself over to you, to be one with you in all things. And I receive all the work and all of the triumph of your cross, death, blood, and sacrifice for me, through which I am atoned for, I am ransomed and transferred to your kingdom, my sin nature is removed, my heart is circumcised unto God, and every claim made against me is disarmed this day. I now take my place in your cross and death, through which I have died with you to sin, to my flesh, to the world, and to the evil one. I take up the cross and crucify my flesh with all its pride, arrogance, unbelief, and idolatry (and anything else that is a current struggle). I put off the old man. I ask you to apply to me the fullness of your cross, death, blood, and sacrifice. I receive it with thanks and give it total claim to my spirit, soul, and body, my heart, mind, and will.

Jesus, I also sincerely receive you as my life, my holiness, and my strength, and I receive all the work and triumph of your resurrection, through which you have conquered sin, death, and judgment. Death has no mastery over you, nor does any foul thing. And I have been raised with you to a new life, to live your life—dead to sin and alive to God. I now take my place in your resurrection and in your life, through which I am saved by your life. I reign in life through your life. I receive your life—your humility, love, and forgiveness, your integrity in all things, your wisdom and discernment, your strength, your joy, and your union with the Father. Apply to me the fullness of your resurrection. I receive it with thanks and give it total claim to my spirit, soul, and body, my heart, mind, and will.

Jesus, I also sincerely receive you as my authority, rule, and dominion, my everlasting victory against Satan and his kingdom, and my authority to bring your kingdom at all times and in every way. I receive all the work and triumph of your ascension, through which you have judged Satan and cast him down, disarming his kingdom. All authority in heaven and on earth has been given to you, Jesus, and you are worthy to receive all glory and honor, power and dominion, now and forevermore. And I have been given fullness in you, in your authority. I now take my place in your ascension and in your throne, through which I have been raised with you to the right hand of the Father and established in your authority. I now bring the kingdom of God and the authority, rule, and dominion of Jesus Christ over my life today, over my home, my household, my vehicles and finances—over all my kingdom and domain.

I now bring the authority, rule, and dominion of the Lord Jesus Christ and the fullness of the work of Christ against Satan, against his kingdom, and against every foul and unclean spirit that have come against me. [At this point, you might want to name the spirits that you know have been attacking you.] I bring the full work of Jesus Christ against every foul power and black art. I bring the work of Christ between me and all people and their warfare. I bind all this from me in the authority of the Lord Jesus Christ and in his name.

Holy Spirit, thank you for coming. I love you, I worship you, I trust you. I sincerely receive you and all the work and victory in Pentecost, through which you have come. You have clothed me with power from on high and sealed me in Christ. You have become my union with the Father and the Son; the Spirit of truth in me; the life of God in me; and my Counselor, Comforter, Strength, and Guide. I honor you as my Sovereign, and I yield every dimension of my spirit, soul, and body, my heart, mind, and will to you and you alone, to be filled with you, to walk in step with you in all things. Fill me afresh. Restore my union with the Father and the Son. Lead me in all truth, anoint me for all of my life and walk and calling, and lead me deeper into Jesus today. I receive you with thanks, and I give you total claim to my life.

Heavenly Father, thank you for granting to me every spiritual blessing in the heavenlies in Christ Jesus. I claim the riches in Christ Jesus over my life today, my home, my kingdom and domain. I bring the blood of Christ over my spirit, soul, and body, my heart, mind, and will. I put on the full armor of God—the belt of truth, breastplate of righteousness, shoes of the gospel, helmet of salvation. I take up the shield of faith and sword of the Spirit, and I choose to wield these weapons at all times in the power of God. I choose to pray at all times in the Spirit.

Thank you for your angels. I summon them in the authority

of Jesus Christ and command them to destroy the kingdom of darkness throughout my kingdom and domain, destroy all that is raised against me, and establish your kingdom throughout my kingdom and domain. I ask you to send forth your Spirit to raise up prayer and intercession for me this day. I now call forth the kingdom of the Lord Jesus Christ throughout my home, my family, my kingdom, and my domain in the authority of the Lord Jesus Christ, with all glory and honor and thanks to him.

Other Books by John Eldredge

The Sacred Romance (with Brent Curtis)

Desire

Wild at Heart

Waking the Dead

Epic

The Ransomed Heart

Captivating (with Stasi Eldredge)

Fathered by God

Love and War (with Stasi Eldredge)

Where Do I Go From Here?

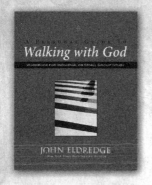

Let John Eldredge guide you personally in your journey to hear the voice of God and walk intimately with Him. In this companion workbook to *Walking with God*, John provides detailed counsel and direction for learning to hear God's voice, and for interpreting what is happening in your life. These questions and reflections will take you deeper into a life of rich intimacy with Jesus Christ!

We all share the same dilemma—we long for life, and we're not sure where to find it. Sooner or later life will break your heart. But do not abandon desire! It is the secret to your heart. You cannot find God or the life he has for you without your heart and its desires!

With *Desire*, embark on your heart's most significant journey—to find the life you are meant to live.

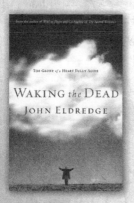

Waking the Dead is a revolutionary book on the human heart, "the wellspring of life" God put in you (Prov 4:23). Here John reveals how the work of Jesus Christ reaches deep into your soul and transforms you into the person God created you to be. Through the "Four Streams" described in this book you will discover not only how God restores your life, but how you can bring restoration into the lives of those you love. "I have come that they may have life," Jesus said, "and have it to the full" (John 10:10).

— Available In Bookstores Everywhere —

FOR THE JOURNEY

DEVELOPING A CONVERSATIONAL INTIMACY WITH GOD

Developing a Conversational Intimacy with God explores why it is part of the normal Christian life to walk intimately with Christ. He longs to speak, and it is our right and privilege to hear His Voice. If you long for more in your relationship with God, you will understand "how" and "why" we are invited into the closest of fellowships with Him.

THE HOPE OF PRAYER

Things Can be Different.

Every one of us can point to things in our lives that we'd sure like to see change. Lots of things. Relationships that need some help. Health issues. A need for guidance and direction. Financial woes . . .

The list for most of us is pretty long. And to help us bring about that change, God has given us prayer.

The Scriptures talk a lot about prayer, but we're not really sure what to do with it, or, more importantly, how to do it. At least, how to do it in a way that works. Meaning, it actually brings about change.

But that's what prayer is supposed to do! Bring about change. When Jesus teaches us to pray "Thy Kingdom come, thy will be done," he means precisely that—that our prayers somehow enable the Kingdom of God to come and his will to be done "on earth as it is in heaven."

Meaning, here, now, in our lives.

In *The Hope of Prayer* series John shares how to pray with hope and confidence—how to apply prayer to the various dilemmas of life. A live audience recording, this 8 CD set includes the question and answer period at the end of each session, as well as, John fielding prayer requests and praying—providing a mini prayer clinic.

There are few thoughts as hopeful as the thought that things can be different. And so the disciples said, "Teach us to pray." We hope through this series you will find answers to many of the questions you have longed to ask.

THE UTTER RELIEF OF HOLINESS

"Long before he laid down earth's foundations, God had us in mind, had settled on us as the focus of his love, to be made whole and holy by his love." (Ephesians 1: 3–4, *The Message*)

Whole and holy. Have we ever put those two words together before? We've thought of wholeness as something for which we hope . . . that remains elusive. And as for holiness, doesn't the word sound sort of heavy and disciplined and hard?

It's not.

When we discover what the salvation of Jesus Christ means for our own restoration, we'll find that holiness is an expression of the healing of our humanity. What a relief it would be to be set free from all that plagues us: the inner struggle with anger or contempt—the struggle with habitual sins.

We can! We can be set free . . . through the healing work of Christ in our lives.

In this four-part CD series, John Eldredge explores the beauty of the genuine goodness available to us in Jesus Christ and guides us through the process whereby God makes us whole and holy by his love.

You will be relieved. Utterly.

Only Available at RansomedHeart.com!